DON'T MISS THESE INVALUABLE BOOKS
BY ELLEN SUE STERN

THE INDISPENSABLE WOMAN

A positive, reassuring, and ground-breaking book that offers a step-by-step recovery program for women who think they have to do it all—and do it perfectly.

"A hard look at the problem of indispensability and perfectionism in women. An enlightening read."
—MELODY BEATTIE, author of *Codependent No More*

"Indispensable for women who want to recover."
—ANNE WILSON SCHAEF, author of
Meditations for Women Who Do Too Much

RUNNING ON EMPTY
Meditations for Indispensable Women

Supportive, succinct thoughts for each day of the year that can help you restore the balance between outer efficiency and the inner, free, spiritual you. Here are meditations on themes such as overachievement, resisting guilt, and nuturing love, sex, and intimacy.

EXPECTING CHANGE

The Emotional Journey Through Pregnancy

Ellen Sue Stern

BANTAM BOOKS
New York · Toronto · London · Sydney · Auckland

None of the stories used in this book is based on any one individual. All names are fictitious and all case histories are of the author's creation based on the composite of her professional experience.

EXPECTING CHANGE
A Bantam Book / published by arrangement with the author

PUBLISHING HISTORY
Poseidon Press edition published 1986
Bantam edition / December 1993

Library of Congress Cataloging-in-Publication Data

Stern, Ellen Sue, 1954–
    Expecting change : the emotional journey through pregnancy / Ellen Sue Stern. — Bantam ed.
        p.   cm.
    Previously pub.: New York : Poseidon, 1986.
    Includes bibliographical references.
    ISBN 0-553-37038-3
    1. Pregnancy—Psychological aspects.   2. Mothers—Pregnancy.
I. Title.
RG560.S74   1993
618.2′4′019—dc20   93-11063
                                                                                         CIP

Published simultaneously in the United States and Canada

Bantam Books are published by Bantam Books, a division of Bantam Doubleday Dell Publishing Group, Inc. Its trademark, consisting of the words "Bantam Books" and the portrayal of a rooster, is Registered in U.S. Patent and Trademark Office and in other countries. Marca Registrada. Bantam Books, 1540 Broadway, New York, New York 10036.

PRINTED IN THE UNITED STATES OF AMERICA
FFG   0 9 8 7 6 5 4 3 2 1

TO GARY,
Through each season, always.

ACKNOWLEDGMENTS

One of the finest rewards of writing this book has been the abundance of love and support which I received from so many people. I wish to thank everyone who was generous with their ideas, time, and encouragement. I hope that each of you will share in the pride of ownership which is rightfully yours. Special acknowledgment goes to the following individuals:

To Gary, my husband and partner, my gratitude for making this a shared dream.

To Zoe and Evan, who make it all matter.

To my four parents, who have been there 100 percent.

To Jonathan and Wendy Lazear, my agents, for believing in this book.

To Jan Magrane, whose creative collaboration on the workshops was the source of many ideas in the book. And my deepest gratitude for your wisdom, vision, and friendship.

To Bonnie Dickel, for your generosity and warmth.

To Dawn Graves, for opening your door and your heart.

To Katherine Mitchell, a rare spirit.

8 ACKNOWLEDGMENTS

To Beverly Lewis, for clarity, insight, and respectful input.
To Pamela Espeland, for editing and improving the manuscript.
And to Rhoda Levin, who makes me excited about starting the
New Year.

CONTENTS

FOREWORD by Niels H. Lauersen, M.D.   15

INTRODUCTION   17

STAGE ONE   23

CHAPTER 1: YOU'RE PREGNANT—
  BUT WHY?   25
  Getting Pregnant: A Matter of Style   26
  Four Reasons for Getting Pregnant   32
    The Desire to Change Your Life   32
    The Desire for Stability   34
    The Longing to Nurture   35
    The Need for Purpose   37
  It's Okay to Feel Ambivalent   38
  Warning: Setups Can Be Hazardous to
    Your Emotional Health   39

For Veteran Mothers   40
For Fathers   41

CHAPTER 2: IT'S ABSOLUTELY,
DEFINITELY POSITIVE!   44
Your Relationships: Breaking the News   46
   Telling the Father   46
   Telling Your Family and Friends   49
   Telling Your Employer and Co-workers   53
For Veteran Mothers   54

CHAPTER 3: THE PERFECT
PREGNANT WOMAN   58
The Superwoman Complex   63
Your Mate's Image of the
   Perfect Pregnant Woman   65
Meet the Perfect Pregnant Woman   66

CHAPTER 4: COPING   69
Your Body: What's Happening?   70
   The Loss of Control   71
   Taking Charge—and Letting Go   73
Handling Unsolicited Advice   78
Sorting Through What You Read and Hear   80
Coping with Your Fears   81
Choosing Your Medical Provider   83
For Single Mothers-to-Be   85

STAGE TWO   89

CHAPTER 5: THIRTEEN WEEKS:
YOU MADE IT!   91
How Are You Feeling, Dear?   92
How You See Yourself   93
How You See Your Mate   95
Dollars and Sense   97

To Work, or Not to Work? 98
Life-style—and Substance 103
Investing Yourself in Your Pregnancy 105
For Over-35 Mothers-to-Be 106

CHAPTER 6: GETTING WHAT YOU NEED 108
Getting in Touch with Your Needs 109
Your Needs and Your Relationships 111
Sure Steps to Meeting Your Needs 113
Identifying Your Feelings 113
Defining Your Needs 114
Creating Solutions 114
Asking for Support 115
Strengthening Your Support Systems 116
Your Mate 116
Your Medical Provider 121
Your Work 122
Negotiating Your Maternity Leave 127
For Medical Providers 129
For Employers 130

CHAPTER 7: "I'M NOT FAT,
I'M PREGNANT!" 132
Feminine or Fat? 134
Whose Body Is It, Anyway? 138
Shopping: A Serious Subject 139
You Look Terrific! 142

CHAPTER 8: IS THREE A CROWD? 144
Sex and Sexuality 144
Staying Close to Your Mate 147
Hidden Agendas 149
For Fathers—From Fathers 152
For Fathers—From a Mother 154

STAGE THREE 155

CHAPTER 9: FACING YOUR FEARS   157
Four Reasons to Face Your Fears   158
Fears About the Baby   160
  Unexpected Endings   163
Fears About the Birth   165
  The Fear of Pain   166
  The Fear of Losing Control   168
  Performance Anxiety   171
  Taking Charge—and Letting Go   171
Fear and Power   174
Fear That the Baby Won't Come   176
Your Best Is Enough   178
For Coaches   179

STAGE FOUR   181
CHAPTER 10: POSTPARTUM: THE BRIDGE   183
The Bonding Myth   185
Coping with the Blues   188
Counting Your Losses   192
Coming Home   196
At-Home Support   199
  Who Should Come?   199
  When Should They Come?   200
  Why Should They Come?   201
Expecting Change   203
Reaping the Rewards   205
Managing Your Time   208
  Setting Priorities   209
  Getting Organized   210
For Veteran Mothers   211
Handling Visitors   212

CHAPTER 11: FROM WOMAN TO MOTHER   216
Changing Lives, Changing Roles   217
  Your Identity   218

Your Relationship with Your Mate 219
Your Profession 220
Your Life-style 221
Your Values 221
"Will I Be a Good Mother?" 222
Remembering Our Mothers 223
Our First Role Models 225
Intimacy and Independence 230
For Grandmothers-to-Be 231
Your Greatest Wish 233
Why Did Your Child Choose You? 235

AFTERWORD 237
CHAPTER NOTES 239

FOREWORD

Pregnancy has never been safer or more exciting. With new insights into fetal development and technological creations such as ultrasound, amniocentesis, and fetal monitoring, today's nine months of bearing a baby have been revolutionized. It is remarkable that early in this century childbirth was still considered a risky business.

The many healthy pregnancies and childbirths experienced today result in great part from the knowledge that women themselves have acquired. Women have learned to be aware of their bodies even before they conceive. More and more, they are looking to their obstetricians to be partners with them in pregnancy, not just overseers of their progress.

I have always encouraged women to understand how much personal control they have over their own bodies. I advise women to strengthen themselves in advance, because pregnancy affects everything—all the major organs, biological systems, and that most elusive entity, the psyche. Pregnancy has profound effects on the mind as well as the body, and no two women respond the same way. Having a baby is a joyful but complicated experience. And while the physical side of pregnancy has been researched and improved by technological breakthroughs, the psychological side, in comparison, has hardly been explored.

Pregnancy is a deeply emotional event, a life-changing passage that defies concise description. An expectant mother has emotional ups and downs, and she experiences sometimes overwhelming feelings as she progresses from trimester to trimester, feelings that spring from many sources and cannot be explained away as "hormonal changes."

I am pleased that Ellen Sue Stern has created a guide through pregnancy's strongly felt, unseen side. *Expecting Change: The Emotional Journey Through Pregnancy* advocates a much-needed awareness of the psychological side of pregnancy. Health-conscious expectant mothers read about the physical changes of pregnancy, what they should or should not do at different stages, how the fetus grows and responds, but they are in the dark about the emotional upheaval they feel. Ellen Sue Stern enlightens women about the different emotional stages of pregnancy—the doubts, fears, and elations of expectancy. The pregnancy experience becomes most fulfilling when a woman is informed, reassured, and supported by her husband, her family, and her physician. As part of the support team, I welcome this book.

Niels H. Lauersen, M.D.
Professor of Obstetrics and Gynecology
New York Medical College
and author of *Childbirth with Love*

INTRODUCTION

The experience of pregnancy may change your life more than anything ever has or ever will. When it's over, the extra weight will disappear and the stretch marks will fade, but the emotional changes will last forever.

I was elated when I learned that I was pregnant. Within days, I had told everyone I knew. I was eager for my body to swell and eager for the attention that surrounds expectant mothers. I assumed that all pregnant women became beautiful, got healthier, and achieved complete contentment.

When the first waves of nausea hit, I welcomed them as a sign of impending motherhood. But my morning sickness sometimes lasted all day, my excitement was tempered by fatigue, and although people *said* I looked beautiful, I missed my waist. And as much as I looked forward to the baby, I was terrified by the thought of labor and delivery.

I began to question how much I really knew about having a baby. Most of my knowledge centered around the notion that pregnancy and childbirth were things that women *just do*. Since all our mothers had been there, I assumed that these were automatic, casual female functions. But if pregnancy was supposed to be simple and easy, why was it consuming all my emotional energy?

I started wondering if other women felt as I did, so I looked around for information and support. Along the way, I discovered amazing new techniques for conception, excellent classes in childbirth preparation, and various options for labor and delivery. Library and bookstore shelves overflowed with facts about nutrition, exercise, and fetal development—the *physical* realities of pregnancy. But nowhere did I find anything that dealt with the *emotional* ups and downs that were as much a part of my experience as the kicking and the heartburn.

I decided to go straight to the source: other pregnant women. I soon learned that *all* expectant mothers have doubts and fears. I have never met one who doesn't worry about her weight gain, fantasize about birth defects, question her qualifications for motherhood, or assume that labor will be worse than people claim. But because there is no forum for airing these concerns, the women keep quiet about them. They don't want to take up too much of their doctors' time or appear to be prima donnas.

When a woman says that she's tired of being pregnant or sick of carrying the baby around, others may question her commitment to the baby or the strength of her maternal instincts. Our culture expects pregnant women to be calm, confident, and secure—modern-day madonnas. In fact, most feel uncomfortable and ambivalent just as often as they feel serene and assured.

During my search, it became clear to me that carrying a child and bringing it into the world *aren't* things that women *just do*. They are not matter-of-fact. They are challenging, rewarding, and life-altering. They influence our relationships and transform our perceptions of the world.

In the nine months of pregnancy, we go through a lifetime of emotions. In childbirth, we participate in the ultimate act of creation. Men spend years, decades—even their entire lives— trying to equal these accomplishments.

Ask any woman who has been there. Even if she's in her

eighties or nineties, she may recall pregnancy and childbirth with clarity and drama. And most women will say that motherhood remains their greatest source of pride and joy.

We're in an age in which test-tube babies and underwater deliveries are the stuff of afternoon talk shows, yet there's little or no mention of the struggles of pregnancy and the triumphs of childbirth. We voice our support for women's rights and are quick to discuss the advances in our careers, but we're silent on the heroics of birth.

Why? Because the universal nature of pregnancy detracts from its importance? Because we take ourselves for granted and downplay our role in the miracle of life?

I believe that *every woman knows* what pregnancy and childbirth really mean. Any woman who has felt her baby's movements, worried about its health, and labored for its life *must* know. I also believe that any man who has witnessed the birth of his child has a heightened appreciation of what women are made of.

It's time to give pregnancy and childbirth the public reverence and respect they deserve. That's part of what this book is all about.

Every pregnancy is unique, but some concerns are common to all pregnant women. *Expecting Change* is divided into three emotional "stages" that correspond to the three trimesters of pregnancy, as well as a fourth stage referring to the postpartum period.

> Stage One begins with the decision to conceive and continues through the end of the third month.

Women in Stage One call the doctor back to double-check the results, buy several books about pregnancy, browse through racks of maternity clothes, and fall asleep in the middle of a sentence. They talk about EPT tests, food, sleep, and the latest remedies for morning sickness. They think about genetics, food additives, pollution, and the possibility of having a miscarriage.

Women in Stage One can hardly believe that they're pregnant.

> Stage Two starts at the beginning of the second trimester and goes through the end of the sixth month.

Women in Stage Two wear oversize sweat shirts, stare at themselves in the mirror, sign up for exercise classes, and gravitate toward other pregnant women. They talk about their checkups, maternity clothes, and monthly weight gain. They think about life-styles, health, the family's income, and whether they're still sexy.

Women in Stage Two have no doubt that they're expecting a baby.

> Stage Three begins with the seventh month and ends with the birth.

Women in Stage Three have bizarre dreams, wear flat shoes, are constantly in the bathroom, and have a calendar next to their bed. They talk about contractions, diapers, maternity leave, and the latest name for the baby. They think about lack of freedom, birth defects, due dates, and what kind of mother they will be.

Women in Stage Three can't remember what it's like not to be pregnant.

The opportunity for personal growth is present in each of these stages. As your baby's birth draws near, you'll be faced with the need to examine your values, explore your relationships, and evaluate your priorities. In doing so, you'll come to a deeper understanding and appreciation of yourself.

I hope that this book will guide, support, and affirm your emotional experience of pregnancy. I have included my own within it—not because it exemplifies the only way or the right way, but in the spirit of shared realities, sisterhood, and the vision of new life.

EXPECTING
CHANGE

Stage One

1

YOU'RE PREGNANT— But Why?

It may seem silly to ask yourself why you're pregnant. Of all the questions you could possibly be wondering about during these turbulent times, that one appears to have the most obvious answer.

You may *think* you're pregnant because you planned it, because the power failed, or because your mate got unusually romantic. Or maybe you went on vacation and forgot your diaphragm. In any case, the *real* reason is that one day not too long ago *you decided to have a baby*.

Do you remember that day? Think back. What were the factors that combined to set in motion one of the biggest changes of your life?

I remember exactly when I decided to have my first child. It was January 12, 1980. Up until that day, I had given little if any thought to becoming a mother. And then, all of a sudden, it was the only thing in the world that mattered.

I went to visit an old friend, Nina, who had just had a baby. I had picked out a cute little gift: a mobile with four fuzzy lambs and a music box that played a lullaby. I stopped by during my lunch hour with no intention of staying any longer than necessary to hand over the gift, exclaim politely over the baby, and say good-bye.

Two hours later I was still there, counting Michael's fingers and toes (from a safe distance) and listening spellbound to the details of Nina's labor and delivery. I finally asked if I could hold him. I was dressed for work in my best silk suit, and I awkwardly arranged myself in Nina's rocking chair and reached out my arms.

Within ten seconds, Michael had spit up all over my shoulder. I couldn't have cared less—which turned out to be my first clue. While Nina rushed around with paper towels and apologies, all I could think about was how much I wanted to have a baby of my own, and nine months seemed like an unreasonably long time to have to wait.

Today I'm the mother of two active and demanding children, Zoe and Evan. Whenever I'm interrupted for the tenth time in a row, or called in to referee a battle over a cookie, or summoned to search for a lost shoe—or any of the other day-to-day, minute-to-minute "crises" mothers face—I still find it helpful to look back and remember how very much I wanted each one of my babies. You will, too.

GETTING PREGNANT: *A Matter of Style*

While your pregnancy began with conception, your *emotional experience* of pregnancy started the moment you first thought about having a baby and decided to do it.

The first step in understanding your emotional experience involves understanding *how* you made that decision. Although there are only a few ways of getting pregnant, there are several different styles of arriving at that point.

What was yours? This quiz can help you find out. Choose the *one* response from each group that seems to apply most closely to you.

1. When I learned that I was pregnant, I was . . .
   A) not at all surprised. I'd planned it down to the moment!
   B) somewhat surprised. I'd thought about having a baby, and had hoped to have a baby, but I'd never really planned it.
   C) surprised. I'd flirted with the idea of motherhood, but I hadn't yet really committed myself to it.
   D) *very* surprised. I couldn't understand how this had happened to me!

2. I felt . . .
   A) very pleased and excited. Things had worked out precisely as I'd wanted them to.
   B) excited and rather pleased. I would have done it sooner or later, and this seemed as good a time as any.
   C) mixed up. On the one hand, I liked the idea of being pregnant, but on the other, I wasn't quite sure that *now* was the time.
   D) shocked. This wasn't *my* decision.

3. I thought that my pregnancy was . . .
   A) terrific. And it fit right into my schedule.
   B) great. I had been dreaming about being a mother someday.
   C) okay. I wasn't quite ready for it, but as long as it had happened, I accepted it.
   D) too much, too soon. Suddenly I'd lost all control over my life.

4. When people asked me how I'd decided to get pregnant, I said . . .
   A) I looked at my calendar and picked a time when having a baby would be most convenient.
   B) I let nature take its course.

    c) I didn't *really* decide. I just figured that getting pregnant wouldn't be the worst thing that could happen.

    d) it was an accident.

Interpreting your score:

> *If you chose all or mostly A answers, it's your style to be a Strategic Planner.*

The Strategic Planner practically writes her delivery date on her calendar before she's even pregnant. (If she's a teacher, for example, she arranges to have her baby in early June. That way she can use the summer for her maternity leave and return to teaching full-time in the fall.) She takes her basal temperature religiously and is up on the most effective times and positions for conception.

Some Strategic Planners consult their astrologers or count backward from Mother's Day. A few target December 31 for the blessed event—to take advantage of the tax breaks.

Talk to a Strategic Planner after she's decided to get pregnant but before the *fait* is *accompli*, and she'll say that she's "working on making a baby," as if it's a job to get done, on time, with no excuses. (Hers is the mate who looks haggard every thirty days or so.)

> *If you chose mostly B answers, it's your style to be an Optimist.*

The Optimist is equally determined to have a baby but considerably more relaxed about the details. She stops using birth control in the hope of eventually conceiving but without a precise date in mind. Rather than scheduling her delivery, she mentally clears her calendar for the next year or so.

The Optimist enjoys daydreaming about herself as a mother. She's a little disappointed if the first and second tries don't work out, but she gives herself at least six months before starting to worry seriously. Meanwhile she doesn't tell people what she's up to; if asked, she likely says, "We're letting nature take its course."

> *If you chose mostly* C *answers, it's your style to be a Gambler.*

The Gambler may not throw money on the table in Las Vegas, or bet on horses, or buy lottery tickets, but she still plays a game where getting pregnant is concerned. Let's call it Baby Roulette.

Her approach to getting pregnant reflects her mixed feelings about being a mother: she likes the idea one day and isn't sure the next. She uses birth control erratically, sometimes throwing caution to the winds. She flirts with the idea without ever really committing herself.

The Gambler may joke about having a baby, but she's very interested in other pregnant women. That's her way of doing research. How will *she* look? How will *she* feel? She thinks that looking at and talking to pregnant women gives her the answers she needs to make a decision.

But she never really decides anything one way or the other. She may not even admit to herself that she wants to have a baby. If someone asks her about it, she'll probably say something like, "It wouldn't be the worst thing that could happen."

> *If you chose mostly* D *answers, it's your style to be an Innocent Bystander.*

The Innocent Bystander gets pregnant "by accident." Maybe she has a little too much to drink, or gets carried away by passion, or neglects to use her birth control "just once." In any event, she avoids taking responsibility for her pregnancy.

She'll claim that it wasn't her decision or, more often, that it wasn't her "fault." When you dig deeper, what you'll find is a wistful desire for a baby combined with a genuine fear of commitment.

The Innocent Bystander starts motherhood with mixed feelings. Fortunately, nine months is usually long enough to get used to the idea and accept it as fact.

None of these four profiles takes into account the complexities of what each of us goes through in deciding to have a baby. They're presented here simply to get you accustomed to thinking about yourself: your motives, your reasons—the new life within you.

The way you approach conception sets the stage for your experience of pregnancy.

- The Strategic Planner is exceedingly well prepared, but she may be disappointed if she gains a bit too much weight, if morning sickness interrupts her normal routines, or if the baby is late. She may need to become more flexible for the next nine months—not to mention the next twenty years!
- The Optimist enters her pregnancy with a positive attitude, but she may be somewhat naive about the realities. While her ability to stay relaxed is an advantage, she may need to become more assertive.
- The Gambler may feel that she's hit the jackpot. She embraces the exciting new direction her life has just taken and looks forward to the challenges ahead. But she may need to stop relying on luck, since she's going to have to start making responsible decisions.
- The Innocent Bystander may view her pregnancy as welcome news or a demanding intrusion. Either way, she'll need to accept her pregnancy and take charge of it (and herself).

Why is the decision to get pregnant so difficult to make? Why is it so complicated? Doesn't it seem that if a woman wants a baby, she should just go ahead and try to have one—that it should be that simple? Why do we spend so many hours and days and months (and even years) thinking about it, discussing it with other people, reading about it, and weighing its countless pros and cons?

All these questions have the same answer: *Because deciding to have a baby means making major life changes.* In today's world, choosing motherhood means reshuffling everything from your closet space to your long-term career goals.

Not too many years ago, women didn't have the freedom of reproductive choice that we now enjoy. Most of our grandmothers, and many of our mothers, did not have the right to decide when and whether they wanted children, or how many children to have. Their options were limited both by the unavailability of safe, reliable birth control and by cultural expectations. Women were supposed to have children. That's what they were put on earth to do.

No longer. Having a baby is definitely a choice today. Women in the 1980s don't automatically get married at age twenty-one, wait two years, quit their jobs, and start birthing babies. There are women who are deferring motherhood until after they've achieved a certain career goal, women who are waiting until their thirties and forties to conceive, women who are opting for single parenthood, lesbian women who are arranging to adopt children or to become artificially impregnated, women who plan to remain childless (the new term is "child-free") forever, women who have terminated pregnancies. There's a whole range of choices that never existed until recently.

There's also a catch. When you know exactly what's expected of you, it's relatively easy to comply. When those expectations aren't as clear, or when they're contradicted by your own wants and needs, things get complicated. For most of us, the decision to get pregnant involves a great deal of soul-searching and examination of priorities.

The main factors involved in this decision usually include age, income, career, and life-style. Julie says that she'll have a baby when she turns thirty, no matter what else is going on in her life at that point. Cynthia vows to do it when she's promoted to vice-president of the company; then she'll have the power and flexibility to take a lengthy maternity leave. Laura insists that she and her husband David will "have a kid when we're ready to quit having a good time." Therese's line of reasoning is the one that's heard most often: "We'll do it when we're financially secure."

On the surface, all these attitudes seem perfectly sensible. But do they actually determine when and whether a woman decides to get pregnant?

I say no. Valid as they appear on the surface, these considerations matter a lot less than women think they do. Although they may have had a definite impact on your timing, no woman ultimately decides to have a baby because she has reached a certain age, received a hard-won promotion, or "settled down," or because the family checkbook balance is finally in the black. When it comes right down to it, the urge to have a baby isn't rational at all.

The *real* reasons behind the decision are tied to your deepest desires and longings for what you most want out of life. You may think these are tied to maturity or timing, fame or fortune; think again.

When you finally decided to have a baby, was there *anything* that could have stopped you? Probably not. With that in mind, let's examine *your* reasons—your *real* reasons.

FOUR REASONS FOR GETTING PREGNANT

The second step in understanding your emotional experience of pregnancy involves understanding *why* you made that decision. This usually involves one or all of the following:

1. the desire to change your life
2. the desire for stability
3. the longing to nurture
4. the need for purpose

Let's look closely at each of these.

The Desire to Change Your Life

If you were, in fact, looking for a way to change your life dramatically, then getting pregnant certainly did the trick! Pregnancy brings change whether you like it or not. Your body changes, your relationships change, your entire identity as a person changes as you undergo the process of becoming a mother.

Which of the following went through your mind when you first considered having a baby?

"If I were pregnant, I could . . ."

1. Improve my marriage.
2. Quit my job.
3. Eat whatever I want.
4. Get my mother (or mother-in-law) off my back.
5. Stop smoking.
6. Be more like my friends.
7. Sleep later in the mornings (and take naps in the afternoons).
8. Move to a (bigger, better, different) place.
9. Get more attention (or sympathy).
10. Stop worrying about who I am.

While it's always possible to make changes in our lives, being pregnant somehow gives us permission to do so. It can also serve as a catalyst for taking stock of where we are and where we want to be.

When baby Michael spit up all over me and set off paroxysms of maternal longing, it wasn't just that I wanted a baby of my own to cuddle. I was looking for a way to get out of the rat race. I fantasized about quiet afternoons peacefully rocking my perfect baby. I didn't think about boredom, dirty diapers, or being broke. I was ready for a big change in my life, and pregnancy seemed like the answer.

Examining your own fantasies can reveal much about what you wanted at the time you decided to get pregnant. Which of these applied to you?

• You hoped that becoming pregnant would spark more interest from your mate or bring the two of you closer together.

- You dreamed about strangers opening doors for you or giving you their seat on the bus.
- You imagined announcing your pregnancy to your parents and having them immediately (and at last) see you as a grown-up.
- You looked forward to a vacation from worrying about your appearance.
- You envisioned your identity changing—from "just you" to "someone's mother."

The bad news, which you may already know, is that pregnancy doesn't automatically bring about the changes you most desire —other changes, surely, but not necessarily the ones you had in mind.

The good news, which you may suspect, is that pregnancy lasts nine months for more reasons than one. It gives you plenty of time to start making changes—positive and meaningful ones that can far surpass your fantasies. If there are things in your life that you really want to change, take this opportunity to do so.

The Desire for Stability

When you first considered having a baby, you may have had thoughts like, "It's time to settle down," or "I want to get my life in order." What you were feeling was the desire to put down roots and anchor yourself to something you could count on.

This may seem to contradict the desire for change; it doesn't. Creating greater stability *is* changing your life.

It's perfectly all right to want stability. Don't misunderstand this as copping out or opting for a predictable, ambitionless existence. Having a baby around will make your life totally unpredictable and filled with countless opportunities to stretch yourself as a person.

Dawn and Peter are in their early thirties and have two children, ages two and five. Here is how Peter explains their reasoning behind starting a family: "Dawn and I had been married for five years when we decided to have our first child. It seemed like the perfect time to move into the next stage of life. For us that meant a family; a home, a garden, a long-term plan. Having children helps us know what we're working for."

Our images of stability stem from our own experiences as children. I grew up behind the famous white picket fence, and I still get nostalgic when I drive past the corner where I waited for the school bus year after year with my neighborhood buddies. In contrast, Karen was an Air Force brat whose family moved at least eight times before she was twelve years old. She was never in one place long enough to develop permanent bonds. She grew much more dependent on her family for her feelings of stability, and she and her sisters learned to lean on one another whenever they moved to a new town.

We all have the urge to recreate our childhood experiences of stability, whatever those may have been. We remember the things that made us feel warm and secure, and we want our children to have them, too.

Whether your image of stability includes a suburban neighborhood, a big city apartment, a farm, or a cabin in the woods, a child probably completes the picture. In fact, emotional stability has very little to do with these kinds of trappings. You've heard the saying that home is where the heart is. What really brings us long-term stability are *the commitments we make to people.*

We all have a need for relationships we can count on. It's the people we love and the people who love us who create the fundamental framework for our feelings of security. Your decision to have a child adds an important element to this framework. By making that decision, you're choosing to build a new and permanent relationship, one that will support and reward you for many years to come. Few things in this world are as certain as a baby's love for his or her mother.

The Longing to Nurture

To nurture means to help something grow. Most of us have some desire to nurture, and we work to fulfill that desire, whether it's by tending a garden, caring for a pet, or raising a child.

When you choose to nurture something, you're making a long-term investment with the hope of eventually reaping the fruits. The investment you make when you decide to have a baby is enormous. You'll spend huge amounts of time, money, energy, and attention in bringing that tiny creature to adulthood (and it won't stop there).

There's a big difference between loving and nurturing. You may love your mate, but you're not in charge of making sure he lives from one day to the next. When you nurture something, on the other hand, you take full responsibility for its well-being. Having a child elevates that responsibility to a whole new level.

When I first brought Zoe home from the hospital, I used to imagine horrible things happening to her. I sometimes envisioned myself putting her in the oven or leaving her outside in the snow. (We live in Minnesota, where winter is no laughing matter.) At first, I was shocked and horrified at the thoughts that popped into my head. I adored my new daughter, and the last thing I wanted was to lose her!

I came to realize that my imagination was performing an important function: playing out the worst possibilities so they could never really occur. As Zoe continued to grow and reached her six-month mark in one piece, my fears gradually diminished until one day they were gone. What remained was an awesome feeling of responsibility, the knowledge that I had given birth to a *new human being* and it was up to me to help her grow.

What makes us willing to take on such a task? What is it about a tiny, dependent infant that makes us feel big and strong and capable of caring for it?

Here's one obvious answer: When you conceive a child, you are recreating parts of yourself. How can a baby with your ears, your eyes, or your smile not tear at your heartstrings? This is not to say that you can't love an adopted child just as much, only that it's natural to be taken with a miniature replica of yourself.

There's also something about a baby's innocence that inspires us to want to care for it. Having a baby gives us the chance to start fresh, to do something right from the beginning, to enter into a brand-new relationship that has no history of problems. The potential to affect an untarnished life is both appealing and exciting.

Finally, we nurture something because we want something from it. Few of us have children merely because *we* want to love *them*. We also want them to love us back. Fortunately for us, they usually do.

The Need for Purpose

Have you ever wondered what it will be like to be seventy or eighty years old? Have you imagined looking back at your life and asking yourself, "What do I have to show for myself? What have I accomplished?

I thought a lot about these things when I decided to have a baby. It was clear to me that a child would add meaning to my life. Not that it was totally devoid of meaning until then; it wasn't. But I wanted something more.

What gives an individual's life meaning or purpose is a deeply personal matter. Wanting a child can be an expression of a spiritual need, a yearning to create something greater than yourself. Bearing a child is the *only* way to "replace" yourself on the planet. You may write a beautiful poem or paint an important picture, and it may or may not live on after you. But a child— that's immortality! Your baby represents a bridge into the future, a means of passing on the heritage, values, and beliefs you hold dear.

Pregnant women often say, "I want to do something that will really matter." The baby isn't the only important part of this process. Often the act of conception in and of itself is ripe with meaning. Many women describe this moment as holy.

Patty, a thirty-year-old executive, explains her decision to have a baby: "A few years ago my best friend was killed in a car accident. For months afterward, I was depressed and distracted. My friends and family eventually grew impatient with me and started saying things like, 'That's enough. Can't you get over this and go on?' But I couldn't shake my despair. It wasn't until I realized I wanted a baby that my depression lifted and I let go of my grief."

She knew that her baby would be an affirmation, a way to start fresh. For her, the tragedy of death opened the door to life.

In choosing to have a baby, you are contributing to the continuation of life on earth. Being part of the cosmic plan and carrying on the chain of human existence is about as meaningful as you can get. What more valuable contribution could you possibly make?

IT'S OKAY TO FEEL AMBIVALENT

It's natural to experience mixed feelings about your decision to have a baby. In fact, ambivalence is a healthy sign that you're aware of the importance of your decision. The responsibilities of pregnancy and motherhood are awesome, and thinking about them should be sobering.

Getting pregnant is a true act of courage. You've chosen to change your life permanently, and any life change takes a huge amount of courage: courage to meet the unknown willingly, courage to make adjustments, courage to grow.

If this will be your first baby, you've entered uncharted territory. Regardless of what others have told you about pregnancy, the experience will still be wholly new for you.

If this is your second, third, or fourth pregnancy (or more), you're facing the equally difficult task of going into this with your eyes wide open, and you're dealing with the added demands of the child or children you're already caring for.

No matter how excited and delighted you are at the prospect of having a baby, I'd be surprised (and somewhat concerned) if you weren't a bit frightened as well. If you were about to move to a new city, you'd probably have mixed feelings of anticipation and apprehension. Often women expect to enter pregnancy with only positive feelings. Don't place that burden on yourself.

All your feelings—from total confidence to abject terror—are perfectly appropriate responses to the changes you're going through. Your ambivalence doesn't mean that you don't want your baby. It *does* mean that you're giving your pregnancy the attention it deserves.

WARNING: *Setups Can Be Hazardous to Your Emotional Health*

The decision to have a baby can be loaded with "setups"—ulterior motives or hidden reasons—and it's important to be aware of these and the dangers they represent. It's also important to be honest with yourself. If any of these descriptions apply to you, it's time to take a long, hard look at what you're doing and why.

- Some women get pregnant in the hope that a baby will "cure" an unhappy marriage.
  It's wrong to expect a newborn to accomplish something two supposedly mature adults haven't been able to do. All a baby can do is provide a distraction and perhaps a temporary respite, but the problems will still be there. In fact, the added stress of having another person (and a very demanding one) around the house will probably make things worse. If your marriage is rocky, get help!

- Some women think that having a baby will introduce "order" into their lives.
  This, too, is placing too much of a burden on the baby. In addition, it just plain doesn't make sense. If you haven't been able to organize your life so far, having a baby won't do it. How can three o'clock feedings, piles of dirty diapers, and twenty-four-hour demands be construed as orderly? Let's face it: babies are disruptive!

- Some women look to their babies to provide them with the love and affection they're not getting elsewhere.
  Unfortunately, they're almost always disappointed. Babies need a lot; they don't give, not for a long time. If what you want is someone else to love rather than someone to love you, you're on the right track. But loving is something we learn by being loved. Surround yourself with friends and relatives who care about you and show it; then you won't need to lean on your baby for support.

While a baby can provide you with a sense of purpose, it shouldn't be your *sole* purpose. Too many mothers have made their children the center of their lives. When the children grow up and move away—which they invariably do (and should)— their mothers are left feeling as if the emotional rug has been pulled out from under them. These are the moms who end up being clingy, demanding, and meddling long after their children have grown up and gone out on their own.

Truly loving our children means eventually letting them go. The less dependent you are on your child to satisfy your needs, the better you will be at loving *and* letting go.

Setups mislead and misguide us. They fill our minds with false hopes and saddle our babies with responsibilities they can't possibly fulfill. If you're expecting your baby to fill gaps in your life, start *now* to make the changes you need to become a more complete person. The healthier you are emotionally, the more you will be able to give your child and the less you will need from him or her.

FOR VETERAN MOTHERS

Women who have gone through three, four, or more pregnancies are living proof that no two are alike. It's one of the few experiences during which you can feel like an expert and a novice simultaneously!

Being pregnant is harder when you already have a child. You get a lot less attention and a lot less rest than you did the first time around. Nobody acts as if it's such a big deal. Everyone has seen you pregnant before. Your doctor may assume that you already have the information you need. You may decide not to take childbirth preparation classes (if you took them during your first pregnancy). You'll probably wear the same old maternity clothes (only earlier). Being pregnant again may easily feel like business as usual, but it's not.

The decision to have another child brings with it a whole new ball game. While you may have been influenced by some or all of the factors discussed earlier, your decision to conceive was probably less the result of a romantic yearning and more of a rational choice.

When we choose to have our first child, just about all we have to guide us are our fantasies and images. When we opt to do it again, we come at it from a new perspective—that of experience. We understand what it's like to be pregnant, undergo labor and delivery, and make the transition to motherhood, and this understanding colors our decision-making. We're likely to feel some ambivalence, but now our mixed feelings are due to what we know.

Maybe you hesitated because you weren't sure that you wanted to go through it all again. The prospect of middle-of-the-night feedings and playpens in the living room can seem like a giant step backward. (One woman put off getting pregnant a second time because her first baby was "so easy," and she was sure she'd never have another as good!)

On the other hand, for many people, there are compelling reasons for having more than one child. Some people's image of a "real family" requires it. They want their son or daughter to enjoy the special closeness of a sibling. And many people look forward to multiplying the rewards of parenthood through one or more repeat performances.

The important thing to remember is that the people around you shouldn't be blasé about your pregnancy just because you're a pro. You may need to remind them that you still need—and deserve—some extra love and attention. Even if you've already had a dozen children, this shouldn't lessen the significance of what you're doing or the amount of respect you receive. The child inside you now is as special as any who came before. He or she is one of a kind—a first.

FOR FATHERS

As an expectant father, your experience of pregnancy will be vastly different from that of your mate. And because men today are far more involved in pregnancy, childbirth, and parenting than their fathers were, you may not have any role models to look to for help in understanding your feelings. That's why you and your mate should take the time to communicate and share your individual points of view.

What did *you* think about when deciding whether to father a child? What went on in *your* mind? What considerations did you weigh? What did you worry about—and what are you worrying about now? Talk about these things! It will be much easier on your mate if she knows what's going on inside you.

When a woman describes why she wants to have a baby, the first thing she usually mentions is the baby itself—how nice it would be to have a little one to love and take care of! Men, in contrast, are likely to talk about *wanting to be a father*. Their desire for a baby seems secondary to their interest in assuming a new role in life.

For most men, the passage into fatherhood signals the symbolic end of freedom and the beginning of genuine responsibilities. Men often joke about having "one last fling" or going on the "final fishing trip" before the baby arrives. But they talk seriously about their income, their future, and their ability to provide for their family.

The belief that one must be the head of the household and the breadwinner has been drummed into *all* the men I have ever met. Even those who are far less role-conscious become very concerned with what's expected of them as soon as they know that a baby is on the way.

Interestingly, however, the main reason most men become fathers is that their mates are ready to have babies. Once in a while, the man will be the one who first broaches the topic, but in the overwhelming majority of cases, it's the woman. This was particularly true in the past, when motherhood was assumed to be every woman's calling. As one seventy-year-old grandfather remembers, "Back when we were having children, it wasn't something you discussed. When Janie said it was time to have a baby, it was time. It wasn't going to disrupt my life, so as far as I was concerned, it was up to her."

Even though men today have a far greater presence in pregnancy and parenting, the decision still rests for the most part with women. This is the way it should be; certainly no woman should be "forced" to have a child she doesn't want.

Chances are that you and your mate made the decision together. Continue to share in the process, and you'll be assured of sharing the rewards.

2

IT'S ABSOLUTELY, DEFINITELY POSITIVE!

There are moments in all our lives that are frozen in time. Our first day of school. Our first period. Our first kiss. Graduation. Our first serious job offer. Our first major fight with our mate. The moment we first learn that our baby is on the way.

I stood there clutching the telephone, my heart pounding, afraid to breathe, knowing that two words—*"It's positive"*—would change my life forever.

"Are you sure?" I asked.

"Yes," said the voice on the other end.

I hung up the phone, rushed to the mirror, and stared into my own eyes. Who was I? Not the same person I'd been five minutes ago. Who was I *now?* The woman in the diaper ad? My next-door neighbor, cuddling her baby on the front porch? My own mother?

I studied myself, searching for a physical counterpart to the rush of feelings I was experiencing. I looked for evidence of change. Was there something different about my expression? A sign of maturity, a glimmer of wisdom, a glow?

Suddenly I panicked. What if I'd heard wrong? Maybe I'd imagined the whole thing! I raced back to the phone and dialed the clinic.

"Did you say positive?"

"Yes."

Total relief!

It would be at least an hour before Gary got home. I didn't know what to do with myself. I tried catching up on some paperwork. I tried straightening up the house. I turned on the television. I turned off the television, got into the car, and headed for Gary's office.

As I automatically lit a cigarette, a thought flashed into my mind: "What about the baby?" What was I going to do about my two-packs-a-day habit? I threw the cigarette out the window. I reached for my seatbelt—which I'd never worn until then—and buckled myself in. I slowed to below the speed limit and started living my life as a mother-to-be.

It's natural to feel shocked and overwhelmed when you find out that you're going to be a mother. Even if you hoped and planned for the baby, the implications of motherhood are so dramatic and far-reaching that they can be hard to absorb all at once.

The moment we learn we're pregnant, something inside us moves. It isn't the baby; it's our own image of reality. We instantly experience the entire spectrum of emotions involved in pregnancy.

We count back three months from the beginning of our last period, add seven days, and mentally calculate our child's birthday. We picture ourselves ripe and swollen at full term. We think about our careers and wonder about maternity leave. We imagine, in colorful and gory detail, what labor and delivery will be like. We daydream about the kind of mother we'll be.

In the first few minutes of pregnancy, we run through the next nine months as if it were a movie in our minds. No wonder we walk around in a daze!

What overwhelms us so is the intense anticipation of change. We know things are going to be different. We know our lives will never be the same.

In each stage of your pregnancy, you're going to experience changes in five areas of your life: your relationships, your body image, your life-style, your fears and anxieties, and your sense of identity. In the chapters to come, we'll be examining how these changes affect your emotions.

YOUR RELATIONSHIPS: *Breaking the News*

Should you or shouldn't you? Tell, that is. You've just found out that you're pregnant, and your life is about to change. Whom should you call? Your mate? Your mom? Should you run next door and proclaim it to your neighbor? Should you get on the PA system and broadcast it to your co-workers? Should you rent a billboard?

As you travel the path of pregnancy, you'll be faced with countless decisions ranging from who your doctor will be to what kind of curtains to hang in the nursery. The first decision is one that comes up immediately: how (and where, and to whom) to make the announcement. On the surface, this may appear to be a simple, concrete decision that has little to do with your feelings. In fact, with whom you share the news, and when, and why are all likely to reflect your feelings very accurately.

Telling the Father

The first person most of us tell is our mate—the father of the child. With very few exceptions, you should include him right from the start. This is his baby, too.

How will he respond? Will he celebrate, or will he let you know in one way or another that your news is less than welcome? Your mate's response will probably be directly related to how you made the decision to conceive. If the two of you happily agreed to try to have a baby, then it stands to reason that he'll rejoice, and you can feel confident about telling him. But if either of you was reluctant to make a baby, both of you may feel uncertain, uncomfortable, frightened, or even angry.

Most of us fantasize about what it will be like to announce our first pregnancy. As far back as I can remember, I imagined the following scenario:

I'd get all dressed up and meet Gary at an elegant restaurant. We'd have a lovely evening—good food, lively conversation, romantic glances across the table. Just before dessert arrived, I'd excuse myself and pretend to go to the women's room. On the way, I'd intercept the waiter and enlist his help. Then I'd go back to the table, and the waiter would bring a glass of champagne for my husband. I'd smile knowingly and tell him to drink up. At the bottom of the glass would be a pacifier with a pink-and-blue ribbon tied around it. He'd break into a grin and throw his arms around me. Everyone in the restaurant would applaud.

It's no secret that life rarely gives us exactly what we hope for. What *really* happened was this:

When I arrived at Gary's office (remember, I had decided to drive there—slowly! carefully!), he was frantically working on a project that was due before the end of the day.

I burst in and blurted out, *"I'm pregnant!* You're going to be a father!"

He stared blankly at me. I repeated myself.

Finally he said, "That's nice." Then he managed a weak smile and asked, "Are you sure?"

"Yes! I'm sure! It's absolutely, definitely positive!"

The next thing he said was that he had to get back to work.

I sat in his office, trying to hold back my tears. Then I got up and drove back home.

Two whole days passed before Gary was able to talk about it. I spent those two days worrying that he didn't want the baby and didn't love me after all. The truth was that he had been totally overwhelmed by the news. He'd needed time to process it before he could express his joy.

This is an important time in your pregnancy. You'll want to share your excitement—and you'll want to be as honest as you can about any negative feelings you're having, especially if your pregnancy wasn't planned. If this is the case for you, you may want to sit quietly and think for a while before telling your mate or anyone else. Try to get a handle on your own feelings before you start stirring up feelings in others.

If your mate's reaction doesn't meet your expectations, give him some rope. You've had a little time to absorb the news; he hasn't. The next nine months (and probably the next twenty years) are playing like a movie in his mind, too. His own images of pregnant women, childbirth, and himself as a father are flashing before him. He may be feeling thrilled, scared, or numb—just like you. Allow him the right to have and express these feelings, and you may discover that you're going through many of the same things.

You and your mate will spend the first trimester just getting used to the idea of having a baby. You'll spend a lot of time talking about your pregnancy and wondering how it will change your life together. It's natural for both of you to feel some fear, trepidation, anxiety, and possibly even regret for the "old days."

You'll worry about how he'll react to you as a pregnant woman. Will he still be attracted to you? You'll wonder about how involved he'll want to get. Will he go through childbirth classes with you? Will he be at the birth?

He'll have questions of his own. How is he supposed to act? What are you going to need from him? Will you still be the same person he knows and loves?

No matter how close the two of you are, no matter how secure you both feel in your relationship, the announcement that you're pregnant is going to shake things up. Count on it.

Andrea is in the middle of her first trimester, and she and her husband Ben have recently started fighting a lot. "He works too much and he comes home too late," she complains. "He leaves his clothes in a pile on the floor. He wants to go on his annual fishing trip and I don't think he should. I used to look forward to having that time to myself, but this is different. It seems like *everything* he does or wants to do is wrong."

Andrea's real fear is that Ben won't be there to help her through the pregnancy and labor, or with the baby after it arrives. She and her husband are both very independent and have little practice in asking each other for help or support; until recently, they haven't needed to. They'll both have to learn to come through for each other.

While the mere presence of a baby will not make or break what you and your mate have together, *how you deal with it may*. Pregnancy intensifies whatever emotions already exist between the two of you. If your relationship is primarily loving and supportive, then parenthood will enhance your intimacy and strengthen your bond. It will also reveal any problems that exist. Normal, everyday emotional and economic conflicts are heightened by the pressures of pregnancy and parenting.

Take the opportunity *now* to confront and resolve any major disagreements or sources of friction. Once the baby is born, you may not have the time or the energy.

Don't, however, use this as an excuse to rant and rave. Be gentle with each other! Read books together about the baby's development, or exchange your fantasies about becoming parents. It's not too soon to start comparing ideas for names. You and your mate are at the beginning of a wonderful journey; you need each other's love and support more than ever.

Telling Your Family and Friends

Announcing your news to your family and friends is like inviting them to participate in your pregnancy. Few people, least of all those who are closest to you, can resist the urge to share their reactions, ask you how you're doing, or even tell you what to do. It's not that they want to interfere (at least, most of them don't); instead, they're genuinely concerned and interested in you and the baby.

It isn't fair for you to let them in and then tell them to go away. For this reason, you'll want to be very careful about whom you invite to share in your pregnancy and when you "send" the invitations.

You may choose to wait for a while before telling anyone other than your mate. This is a special time for the two of you, and you may want to keep it private and sacred for as long as you can. There's no reason to rush into making it public.

You may also decide to wait until you feel completely secure about the baby. Sometimes it's hard to predict how other people will react. When Debra told her mother, she expected her to be ecstatic; instead, she responded with the classic comment, "Maybe you shouldn't tell anyone yet. You never know what can happen." That took the wind out of Debra's sails!

All women worry about miscarriage during the first trimester. If having to tell people bad news (in the unfortunate—and statistically unlikely—event that this happens) will add to your grief or make you uncomfortable, then you'd be wise to wait until you're out of the woods. For most women, that's around week 13.

If you're awaiting the results of amniocentesis, a test that is conducted fourteen to sixteen weeks after the last menstrual period, you may want to be especially careful about your timing. Some women base their decision to continue or terminate pregnancy on those results, which are not obtained until approximately four weeks later. You may wish to postpone your announcement until you're completely sure. This depends on how well you know yourself and your own capacity to deal with grief. Perhaps you take comfort from having other people around when you're hurting; perhaps you prefer to go it alone. If you feel that telling people at this stage poses too great an emotional risk, don't do it.

Most women tell their immediate family shortly after telling their mates. Your baby will be their grandchild, niece, nephew, or cousin, so they have a stake in what you're going through. In a very real sense, the baby belongs to them, too.

Take a few moments to prepare yourself before breaking the news to your parents. Try to imagine how they'll react when they hear that you (their "little girl") are about to be a mother and they're about to be grandparents, maybe for the first time. Are they likely to be loving and supportive, or is it possible that they'll respond in a way that will disturb you or put you on the defensive?

In our youth-conscious (make that youth-worshipping) culture, nobody wants to be reminded that he or she is growing old. There's something about the word "grandparent" that conjures an image of gray hair, a cane, and bifocals. If you're producing the family's first grandchild, your parents may not be immediately enthusiastic, even if they've been hounding you for years to have a child. Try to understand this, and give *them* time to adjust.

Family relationships are by nature complex because there's so much history to them. If your parents approve of your mate and are confident of your ability to care for a baby, they'll probably be thrilled (sooner or later) about your pregnancy. Most of our parents really do look forward to having grandchildren—those wonderful little creatures who *aren't their responsibility.*

On the other hand, if your parents question how mature you are, or if they're worried about your economic stability, they may rain on your parade by saying so. Even if they're truly pleased about the news, they may still voice their fears and concerns about your health and your baby's well-being and future.

You know best how your own parents will react. If you trust them to share in your joy in a positive way, then by all means let them in as soon as you can. The more people you have rooting for you, the better. But if you suspect that your parents' reaction is likely to annoy you, hold on to your news for a while. The most important thing right now is to concentrate on *your* needs, not theirs.

The same goes for your friends. While they don't have the same investment in the baby that your relatives do, they, too, may or may not be supportive. You'll need to decide which ones to invite to your pregnancy. Who will be willing to listen to you, and who will insist on giving you unwanted advice? Who will be genuinely interested in the changes you're going through, and who will be threatened by your new identity as a pregnant woman?

You may find that friends who are pregnant or already have children will be more supportive of your pregnancy. They have something else in common with you now, and they're probably more tuned in to how you're feeling. Then again, they may try to relive their own pregnancy through yours. Susan, pregnant for the first time, had this problem with her friend Liz: "Whenever I tried to talk about my pregnancy, Liz would interrupt to reminisce about hers. When I said that I'd already gained twenty-one pounds, Liz warned me that she'd gained thirty and they hadn't come off easily. When I mentioned my preference for unmedicated childbirth, Liz went into raptures about the cervical block she'd been given during transition. What I needed was an ear; what I got was a lecture!"

Friends who have never been pregnant or who have decided not to have children may have difficulty relating to what you're going through. They may also be afraid that once you have the baby, you won't have the time or the desire to continue your relationship with them. Let them know that you want them to share in your experience. Reassure them of their continuing value in your life.

There are many reasons you should try to maintain these friendships. Once you're a mother, it can be a welcome relief to spend time with someone who couldn't be less interested in diapers or nap times. Talking to people who *don't* have kids is a wonderful way to broaden your identity and remain open to other interests. And some of them may be eager to be honorary aunts or uncles to your child.

Chances are, though, that other friends will lose interest or drift away during your pregnancy. This can be painful, but sometimes it can't be helped. Be particularly sensitive to the friend who is having trouble conceiving. Her frustration and disappointment may make it difficult or even impossible for her to remain close to you.

Regardless of whether they have children, friends can be a special part of your pregnancy. One may be a great listener who truly wants to hear every detail of your baby's development; another may invite you to her exercise class or help you to improve your diet. Be very specific about the roles you want them to play. Set limits—or open the door all the way.

Of course, there will be some people you *won't* want to have around. It's your pregnancy, and you don't have to share it with everyone.

What you don't—repeat, *don't*—need are horror stories—grisly accounts of labors that lasted two weeks, false labor alarms, tales about demonic doctors and insensitive nurses. Let it be known that you're not interested.

Telling Your Employer and Co-workers

Once the news is out with family and friends, you'll be faced with another task: telling your employer and co-workers. If you work outside the home, then this is a significant step indeed. You spend a lot of time at your job, and how you feel about yourself in the workplace affects all areas of your life.

Again, the most important factor to consider is how much support you can expect. How do you think your employer and colleagues will react to your pregnancy? Are they likely to be sympathetic and understanding, or will telling them simply add to the pressure you're already experiencing? Will your pregnancy jeopardize your standing—and do you care?

When Amy became pregnant, she was working as an account executive at a radio station—one of two women on a sales force of eight. Her job involved long hours, intense competition, and a high degree of stress. "I debated over how soon to spill the beans to my sales manager," she says. "Unable to contain my enthusiasm, I told him right away. The first words that came out of his mouth were, 'When will you be leaving?' Almost as an afterthought, he added, 'Congratulations.' I wished I'd kept my mouth shut and waited until I was showing!"

You may be torn between the desire to protect yourself and your feelings of responsibility toward your job. You may be justifiably worried about how the news of your pregnancy will affect your current career status and future job security. Some progressive employers will be genuinely pleased for you and will do everything in their power to facilitate your choice (if this is your choice) to continue working now and return after the baby arrives. Others, let's face it, will be real stinkers.

Try to find out what has happened in the past—your employer's customary behavior concerning pregnant women. Talk first to co-workers who have themselves been pregnant and ask them to describe their experiences. What did they do? How were they treated? Do they have any advice for you? Armed with this information, you'll be able to approach your employer with self-confidence and reasonable expectations.

Then again, you may be the trailblazer in your company. Your employer may never have had to deal with a pregnant employee before. Such a thought had never occurred to Anne until she went to her boss, announced that she was pregnant, and asked about maternity leave policies. He replied, "What maternity leave policies? Nobody has ever taken maternity leave before!" This was a twenty-year-old company with sixty employees, mostly men and older women with grown children, and the situation had never arisen.

Anne realized that she had just been given the opportunity to set policy for herself and for others who would come after her. She volunteered to research what other companies of comparable size were doing and to report back to her boss. Then the two of them sat down together and hammered out a maternity leave policy. It didn't include some of the benefits that major corporations can afford, but it was pretty decent nevertheless.

What should *you* do? Whatever you think will be best for you and contribute most to your comfort and security. But don't concern yourself overly with feelings of responsibility toward your job. Yes, it's important. Yes, you need the income. Yes, you enjoy your work, and it contributes to a healthy self-image. But right now, at this moment, there's something else going on in your life, something that demands your attention and requires you to assume an even greater responsibility.

If you quit work today, your company would probably survive without you. But you're all your baby has.

FOR VETERAN MOTHERS

The first time around for anything evokes excitement and anticipation. The second (or third, or fourth, or tenth) may arouse different responses. Since you've been pregnant before, you may not be as amazed or as full of wonder now as you were the first time. You've already traveled this road, and many of the landmarks are familiar.

Still, every child is a gift. Each pregnancy deserves to be greeted with joy. The baby you're carrying today is just as important as any other and should be treated with equal consideration.

Even if you know this, the people around you may not. Women often complain that their mates don't show them enough attention and consideration during subsequent pregnancies. There are several reasons for this, most of which have very simple underlying causes: lack of time and lack of energy.

When you already have one child or more, life is in constant motion. Raising kids takes a lot out of you and your mate and leaves you with fewer opportunities to be alone together. During your first pregnancy, the two of you probably had the leisure to share your feelings and focus much of your mutual attention on the baby and your pregnancy. Those days are gone for good.

Is this a loss or a gain? That depends on you. On the one hand, things aren't the way they used to be, and you may be nostalgic for those earlier, easier times. On the other, your life has already been enriched by at least one child. Would you *really* want to go back and start all over again?

If you're tempted to answer both yes and no, you're not alone. Most of us have mixed feelings when we learn that another child is on the way. We like the way things are; the status quo is comforting. Bringing another baby into the house changes everything. We worry about how it will affect our life-style and our relationships, especially with our other child(ren).

Where will we find the inner resources, not to mention the financial ones, needed to take care of another person? Will we be able to love the new baby as much as the first? Will we have to hire two baby-sitters whenever we want to go out? How will our other children react? Will we ever have a moment to ourselves?

These are important issues to discuss with your mate. If you can't find the time, *make* the time. Don't be afraid to ask for what you need. A second pregnancy isn't business as usual, and you shouldn't have to go through it with any less love and support than you received during your first.

Once you've made the decision to increase the size of your family, when should you break the news to your friends and relatives? You've already carried one child to full term, which means you probably have less fear of miscarriage and more overall confidence. Go ahead and make the announcement earlier this time, if it feels right to you. There's an advantage to letting others in at the beginning: They'll be able to help you longer.

Be prepared for mixed reactions. The second or third time around, people are apt to make insensitive remarks like, "Again?" "Aren't you jeopardizing your career?" or "When are you going to stop?" Some of these comments may provide grist for meaningful conversations; others should be ignored. You don't need to justify yourself to anyone but yourself.

The first trimester can be particularly exhausting. You may be tired; you may be cranky. People are more apt to understand if they know what's going on. I found it a real blessing to have caring people around from the start.

If you haven't yet done this, you may be wondering when to tell your other children. Should you do it immediately and give them ample time to get used to the idea, or should you wait until later? Some children needs lots of advance notice; others can't cope with months of anticipation.

Base your decision at least partly on the child's age. Children are able to grasp different types of information at different stages of their development. If you aren't feeling well, or if you're having to make obvious changes in your routines, you may want to tell your child(ren) early so they'll understand why you're behaving so differently. Even the youngest child can be surprisingly flexible and even sympathetic.

Whenever and however you choose to break the news, take special care to reassure your child(ren) that nobody can ever replace them. You may need to emphasize this over and over, since they're likely to feel some anxiety and insecurity. They'll worry about themselves, and they'll also worry about you, especially if you're under the weather.

You may want to take a special trip to your local library or bookstore; there are numerous excellent books available for siblings-to-be. My personal favorite is the Care Bears' *A Sister for Sam* by Evelyn Mason (Parker Brothers, 1983). It acknowledges the many feelings your child(ren) may be experiencing and lets them know that these feelings are normal. Another suggestion: check to see if your hospital or clinic offers a program to help all of you through this time. Many do, especially those in larger cities. They're usually run by people who are expert at answering children's questions and calming their fears.

The bottom line, as always, is *trust yourself*. You love your child(ren) very much, and naturally you feel protective toward them. You don't want anything to upset their equilibrium or threaten their security. But you're going to *have* to tell them, sooner or later! When you do, keep this in mind: Although your pregnancy may be cutting into the time and energy you usually devote to them, it's also allowing you to give them something valuable in return—a brother or sister to have and love forever.

3

THE PERFECT
PREGNANT WOMAN

Long before you ever conceived, you probably pictured yourself as a pregnant woman. You had a clear image of how pregnant
women look, act, and feel. Now that you're one of them, are you
living up to your ideal?

We all know that there's no such thing as the Perfect Pregnant
Woman. Yet we all know exactly who she is. She's the one who
exercises, eats health foods, doesn't smoke or drink, looks vi-
brant, and only shows in front. Her mate is supportive, her employer is sympathetic, her mother is proud, and her doctor is
always on time for appointments.

Maybe for you the Perfect Pregnant Woman is Princess Di,
Jaclyn Smith, or your next-door neighbor. Maybe she's your best
friend; maybe she's your mom. And maybe she's a wholly myth-
ical figure: the fairy-tale princess you've always wanted to be.

What's *your* image of the Perfect Pregnant Woman? This quiz
can help you find out. Choose the *one* response from each group
that seems to describe her most closely.

1. The Perfect Pregnant Woman . . .
   A) buys a brand-new designer maternity wardrobe
   B) wears India-print smocks and drawstring pants
   C) lives in jeans and oversize sweat shirts
   D) wears anything as long as it's comfortable and clean

2. The Perfect Pregnant Woman . . .
   A) keeps a dog-eared copy of *Spiritual Midwivery* by her bedside
   B) ignores everything she reads about pregnancy
   C) borrows the books that her friends recommend
   D) reads all the latest pregnancy books

3. The Perfect Pregnant Woman . . .
   A) works at a stable nine-to-five job
   B) works only until the baby comes
   C) works herself to death in the hope that she'll be promoted before the baby comes
   D) works for herself

4. The Perfect Pregnant Woman . . .
   A) lives on gourmet take-out foods
   B) eats three wholesome, balanced meals a day
   C) makes her own tofu-molasses cookies
   D) eats whatever satisfies her cravings

5. The Perfect Pregnant Woman . . .
   A) has a midwife who makes house calls
   B) hires a highly recommended specialist
   C) shops around for a medical provider
   D) sees whoever is available at the clinic

6. The Perfect Pregnant Woman . . .
   A) never misses her weekly exercise class
   B) dances to her own beat

c) belongs to a hip health club

d) retreats to the woods to meditate

Scoring

Give yourself the following points for your answers:

1. A	10	B	8	C	6	D	4
2. A	8	B	4	C	6	D	10
3. A	6	B	8	C	10	D	4
4. A	10	B	6	C	8	D	4
5. A	8	B	10	C	4	D	6
6. A	6	B	4	C	10	D	8

Now add up the points to arrive at your total.

Interpreting your score:

51–60 points:
The Perfect Pregnant Professional Woman

This is the woman on the move. She rises early and is impeccably groomed when she arrives at her high-powered job. She doesn't let anything interfere with her demanding life-style; in fact, she manages her pregnancy in the same brisk fashion as her job. She's motivated, organized, and highly energetic.

The Perfect Pregnant Professional Woman signs up early for her childbirth preparation classes and immediately starts interviewing prospective baby-sitters or day-care providers. Being informed is very important to her. She's read everything that's ever been published about pregnancy, and she wants the best medical care available for herself and her baby.

At the conference table or in the labor room, the Perfect Pregnant Professional Woman strives to keep things under control. She hopes that her baby will arrive *exactly* on its due date so that all the elements in her busy life will stay neatly in place.

43–50 points:
The Perfect Pregnant Earth Mother

Mellow is her motto. She believes that pregnancy is a natural state and prefers to keep medical intervention to a minimum. She takes her cues from the baby and attempts to "go with the flow."

The Perfect Pregnant Earth Mother is committed to a healthy diet and will proudly show you her beautiful belly. Today she's wearing loose-fitting, all-natural-fiber clothing; later she'll wear the baby in a cotton pack on her chest.

The Perfect Pregnant Earth Mother will give birth among friends—in a birthing room, at home, or beneath the stars.

33–42 points:
The Perfect Pregnant Girl-Next-Door

This is the most "typical" Perfect Pregnant Woman, and you probably know someone just like her. She's as wholesome as Mary Tyler Moore, as funny as Lucille Ball, and as cute as Sally Field.

The Perfect Pregnant Girl-Next-Door would rather talk about pregnancy than almost anything else. She's eager to give you an up-to-the-minute account of her weekly weight gain, her doctor's schedule, and possible names for the baby. She still hasn't decided precisely what she'll do when the baby comes; she'd like to stay home with it, but she's worried about being away from work too long.

The Perfect Pregnant Girl-Next-Door depends on her friends to share their maternity clothes, books, advice, and stories of labor and delivery. She thinks about childbirth constantly and follows her doctor's orders to the letter.

24–32 points:
The Unconventional Perfect Pregnant Woman

This is the least typical Perfect Pregnant Woman. She's extremely independent and unusually confident. She gathers information from a variety of sources, but nothing influences her very much and she never worries about what other people think.

The Unconventional Perfect Pregnant Woman eats what she wants, sleeps when she's tired, and exercises when she's in the mood. She prides herself on being a well-educated consumer, so she investigates the Childbirth Education Association (CEA), finds out about the Lamaze and Bradley methods of childbirth, and interviews several doctors or midwives until she finds one she likes. She may go through labor wearing her favorite T-shirt and listening to music she's chosen especially for the occasion. And she'll name the baby when she sees it.

One of these four types may fit your image of the Perfect Pregnant Woman; more likely she is a blend of the qualities you most admire. The point is, you're probably comparing *yourself* to your image. You may be pleased to discover the ways in which you resemble her—and surprised or disappointed by the ways in which you don't.

Your picture of the Perfect Pregnant Woman can help you see how your pregnancy is living up to your expectations. Whether or not you knew it, you began your pregnancy with definite ideas of things to come. But reality is usually another story.

Your desire for specific guidelines may lead you to take too literally what you read. For example, you may have seen somewhere that women don't start showing until the fifth month—but you're only eight weeks along and already you're bursting out of your jeans. The art books depict madonnas with beautifully rounded stomachs, but when you look in the mirror, all you see is a woman without a waistline.

Books and articles about pregnancy can give you *general* information, not absolutes. If you measure yourself against everything the books tell you, you're bound to feel let down. Especially when it comes to the physical changes of pregnancy, there are countless exceptions to the rule. Some women are able to wear their prepregnancy wardrobe for a number of months, while others need maternity clothes in the first trimester.

Healthy weight gain can range from as little as fifteen pounds to as much as fifty, and it usually comes in spurts rather than gradual increments.

Your expectations extend into other areas of your life as well. Maybe your pregnant best friend bounced her way through aerobics classes. You swore you'd do the same, but it's taking every ounce of energy you have to stay awake through dinner. Or maybe you heard via the grapevine that an increased sex drive is one of the side benefits of pregnancy, and you'd rather vacuum.

There's nothing wrong with good intentions, but it's equally important to be realistic about your limitations. Why make promises that you may not be able to keep? Especially during the first trimester, when your body is going through so many changes, why not take it easy? Rather than striving to emulate your image of the Perfect Pregnant Woman, remember: she's only an ideal.

THE SUPERWOMAN COMPLEX

Nobody's perfect. Yet we all have images of what "perfection" entails, and we strive toward these images in our own peculiar ways. We're quick to criticize ourselves, and we're hardly ever satisfied.

There was a time, not too long ago, when being pregnant was the best excuse for staying home, resting, and preparing for motherhood. Pregnancy gave a woman nine months to take care of herself and get ready for the baby's arrival. But times have changed, and so have our expectations (and society's) of what a pregnant woman ought to be and do.

Nowadays you're supposed to manage a lucrative career, a meaningful marriage, and a whirlwind social life while simultaneously cooking like Julia Child and staying in shape. You think you're happily married, but every magazine you open is telling you how to "work" on your marriage. Your mother stayed home when she was pregnant with you, but you're up to your ears in office politics. You're satisfied with your appearance—until you start shopping for maternity clothes.

The message is clear: Being a woman today is a big job. The heat is on to be Superwoman.

Few of us are completely at ease with ourselves when we're *not* pregnant. The pressures of pregnancy make matters worse. As your body expands to make room for the baby, your expectations stretch to include the new role of mother-to-be. You're trying to be everything you were and then some, but with less energy than you had before.

You're worried, right? If it's any consolation, there's never been a woman who didn't compare herself to some unreachable standard. I've spoken with hundreds of pregnant women; I've yet to meet one who considers herself the Perfect Pregnant Woman. Most harbor secret fears of not measuring up.

There's another side to this issue: We all want to feel special, but none of us wants to feel *different.* On the one hand, you enjoy fancying yourself as the Original Pregnant Woman, making your mark in the wilderness; on the other, the mere suggestion that your pregnancy deviates from the norm sends you into a tailspin of anxiety and self-doubt. One minute you're sailing along without a hitch, and the next a casual remark about your eating habits has you dialing your doctor for reassurance.

While there's no such thing as the "typical" pregnancy, there is one thing that all pregnant women share: the desire to do it right.

What are *your* hopes and expectations for *your* pregnancy? One way to get in touch with these—and make them available to reflect on later—is by keeping a journal.

Your journal can be a special place—a retreat and a record of what you're going through. You may choose to share it with your mate as a way of helping him understand your experience of pregnancy, or you may want to keep it strictly private. That's up to you. In any event, you should approach it with the intention of letting your thoughts and feelings flow, without judging or censoring anything you write. Your primary purpose should be one of discovering more about yourself.

Here are some questions to get you started. Jot down brief answers or write whole pages; it's *your* journal.

- Do you spend a lot of time worrying? What do you worry about?
- Do you find yourself staring at other pregnant women? How do you compare to them? What do they have that you don't —and vice versa?
- How often do you feel guilty about your diet? Your job? Your relationships? The baby? (Anything else?)
- Do you ever catch yourself smiling for no apparent reason? Are you secretly—or openly—proud of being a pregnant woman?
- Is being pregnant what you thought it would be? What do you like most about it? What do you like least? What things do you wish you could change?
- On a scale of 1 to 10, how well do you like yourself right now? What would it take to think of yourself as the Perfect Pregnant Woman?

YOUR MATE'S IMAGE OF THE PERFECT PREGNANT WOMAN

For you, the Perfect Pregnant Woman is someone else—a princess, a movie star, a relative. For your mate, though, the Perfect Pregnant Woman is supposed to be *you*.

Are you fulfilling his expectations? Or, backing up a few steps, is this something you should even concern yourself with? The answer to that last question is *yes*.

You should at least know what his expectations are, and the best way to find out is by asking. Maybe he's heard that pregnant women are moody and temperamental, which would explain why he's been tiptoeing around you. Maybe he thinks that pregnant women are perpetually blissful, and that's why he's been reacting so strangely to your attacks of the blues.

Before I got pregnant, our friend Lauren was the only pregnant woman Gary had ever spent much time with. His first impressions of how pregnant women acted and felt came from her.

Had there been a Perfect Pregnant Woman contest, Lauren would have taken first prize. Not only did she look lovely and feel great during her pregnancy, she actually loved being in labor!

Naturally, he had high hopes for me. And what did I do? I sat on the couch in front of the TV, too nauseated to lift a finger.

Most of the time, he was terrific. He took care of everything, including me, while I moaned and kvetched about how miserable I was. He never said a word until I was about seven months along. Then one night he casually told me about a dream he'd had about a beautiful woman with a flat stomach.

"How interesting," I remarked, trying to act nonchalant while resisting the urge to smack him. "What do you think your dream meant?"

Six months of resentment came pouring out of him. He had expected a healthy, happy, glowing wife. With my sunken eyes and gray-green complexion, I had shattered his image.

The old saying, If you can't say something nice, don't say anything at all, doesn't apply here. Silence can do more harm than telling the truth. If you share your expectations and images with each other, you may discover some ways in which you're disappointing each other—and do something about them. If you don't, you both may end up feeling tense and uncomfortable without knowing the cause.

Nine months is a long time to keep things hidden. Getting them out in the open *now*—and forming the habit of frequent and regular communication—can prevent the buildup of ill will and misunderstandings. You may even be able to laugh at yourselves, which is often the first step toward acceptance.

MEET THE PERFECT PREGNANT WOMAN

If you *really* want to meet the Perfect Pregnant Woman . . . look in the mirror. Whether you're single or married, rich or poor, career-oriented or not—none of this matters. The

Perfect Pregnant Woman looks like you, acts like you, and feels like you do.

So you forget to take your prenatal vitamins once in a while. So you occasionally grab a doughnut on the way to work. So you're already three pounds too heavy, and you're tired of having to alternate between the gray dress with the white collar and the denim jumper. So what!

How could you possibly be the Perfect Pregnant Woman? Because your pregnancy is the perfect one for you. And the baby you're carrying is the only one that matters.

It may be hard to think of yourself in such glowing terms. If you were just starting a job with no experience whatsoever, you'd feel less than adequate and certainly far from perfect. Being pregnant is no different. Each of us learns how to do it, over time and in our own ways. We try on and get used to a whole new identity. We acquire a new set of skills.

You may wish you were more like Princess Di, Jaclyn Smith, or your next-door neighbor, but you can bet that each of these women had her own issues to deal with. Right now you need every ounce of energy you can muster. Why spend it worrying about whether you're measuring up to anyone but yourself? Instead, try focusing on what a wonderful job you're doing. Naturally you'll make some mistakes along the way; resist the urge to beat yourself over the head when you do. Throw away any yardsticks, real or imagined, that you're using to gauge yourself and your pregnancy. The only worthwhile standard is the way *you* feel.

If you look in the mirror and like what you see, good for you. If you don't, look more closely and try to discover what's troubling you. You may want to consider talking things over with someone you trust and respect—a counselor, your doctor, your rabbi or minister. Or anyone else with whom you can openly discuss your negative feelings.

If you like yourself on some days and not on others, join the crowd! Having doubts during pregnancy is par for the course. What it means is that you're tuned in to the emotional changes you're experiencing. You're a real person, and real people have ups and downs.

You know, of course, that perfection isn't *really* your goal. Instead, you should aim for accepting and appreciating yourself. And never forget the miracle you're bringing into being. Even in the darkest moments of my pregnancies, I always found it helpful to concentrate on the baby.

On the outside, you're just another woman with a newly pregnant body. On the inside, you're a creator. That tiny seed of life is the closest thing to perfection on earth.

4

COPING

Remember the time *before* you were pregnant? You probably had your hands full then—with a home, a mate, a job, relatives, friendships, and all the other responsibilities and obligations that combine to make a full life.

And then you heard the words, "It's positive!"

For a while, everything else faded into the background in the glare of that news. Every ounce of your awareness was focused on the spot inside your body where a baby was beginning to grow.

But you had to emerge sometime. And when you did, you found that none of your prior responsibilities and obligations had gone away. Instead, you discovered that you were carrying an entire roster of additional ones.

You had thought you were coping before. Suddenly that word has taken on a whole new meaning.

YOUR BODY: *What's Happening?*

How many people are you now—one or two? It's close to impossible to comprehend the fact that there's another person living and growing inside you. How can it be? What does it mean? What should you do?

One of the first emotions a pregnant woman experiences is utter amazement. Even though you know how your baby got there, it's still very hard to believe. You may wonder how anything so minute can be real.

Nevertheless, you experience a deep and profound awareness from the moment you know you're pregnant. Suddenly you're *not* the same person you were. You're something more.

Then, too, if you're like most women, you probably are experiencing one or more of the physical signs of pregnancy—nausea, sore breasts, tiredness. Pregnancy is a drain on your body's resources. Your sensations may range from mild queasiness and fatigue to flat-on-your-back exhaustion and debilitating nausea. While there are many women who feel fine during the first trimester, most of us are somewhat out of sorts. Few of us have no physical reactions at all.

It's very common to be especially sensitive to your body's needs during the early weeks and months of pregnancy. You'll actually begin developing a new relationship with your physical self that will continue through your pregnancy and culminate in childbirth. Women in their first trimester are typically concerned with their diet, health, and fitness. Junk-food lovers find themselves reading labels for information on ingredients and nutritional values. Workaholics arrive home promptly at six P.M. and think twice about heading for the office on weekends. Social drinkers switch to spring water or ginger ale. Even the most addicted smokers may take one last puff and throw their cigarettes away. The baby is a compelling motivation for getting serious about your health.

Fortunately there's an abundance of information available on how to get healthy and stay healthy during pregnancy. It's not at all difficult to become well informed. But be alert: Some of what you find out may contribute to your feelings of anxiety and stress. You'll remember that champagne you drank on your anniversary, the rare steak you ate before you realized you were pregnant— or before you realized that undercooked meat could be danger- ous to your baby.

Most first-trimester women express numerous fears and con- cerns. Should they or shouldn't they run the marathon? How many vitamins should they take? Will it really be possible to drink so much milk? What *is* a "leafy green vegetable," anyway?

Everyone frets. *No one* can do it all, know it all, or get every- thing right. Not even you.

But it is important—*very* important—to take care of yourself for your baby's sake. The healthier you are, the greater the chance that your baby will end up healthy. Doing something— anything—is better than doing nothing.

I know from experience how hard it is to worry around the clock. I'll always be grateful to my friend Jeffrey, who told me early on, "You're doing the best you can." His words were a gentle reminder to stop pushing myself—and it's advice worth repeating. Be as knowledgeable and aware as possible—and then do the best you can. If you can't tolerate milk, eat or drink something else that provides similar nutrients. If you miss a day of exercise, try again the next. Your're going through so many changes and making so many adjustments that the last thing you need is to feel as if you're falling short of the mark.

The Loss of Control

There are few times in your life when your body is less your own than when you're pregnant. Do you sometimes hear a little voice saying, "Eat more vegetables," "Put out that cigarette," or "Time for a nap now?" It may seem as though the microscopic creature inside you is running the show.

Well . . . it is.

Most of us are used to being in control of our bodies. We're accustomed to deciding what to eat, whether to smoke, when to sleep, and how much to exercise. When we're pregnant, however, many of these decisions are made for us. And that can be hard to take.

Suddenly you're moving at half-speed when you've always been a high-energy person. Or you have the overpowering urge to take a nap in the middle of the workday. Or you're overcome by motion sickness while sitting perfectly still.

Normally you'd call your doctor or go to bed. Our past experience leads us to associate such feelings with illness.

But *pregnancy is not an illness*. In fact, it's just the opposite. Growing a baby is one of the healthiest and most basic of all life processes.

Nevertheless, you may be having mixed feelings about how much the baby is taking from you. Its needs are competing with yours, and you're constantly making sacrifices on its behalf. And this is only the beginning. As your pregnancy progresses, you'll have even more to cope with, from weight gain and discomfort all the way to the rigors of labor and delivery.

Thea describes how she felt during the first weeks of her pregnancy: "I couldn't keep my eyes open. No matter what I was doing, all I really wanted to do was curl up and go to sleep. I'd be in an important meeting at work and I'd have to pinch myself to stay awake. Or we'd be out having dinner with friends and long before the evening was over I'd start begging to go home. I felt like a big, boring blob. If the baby needed this much attention now, at this early stage, I couldn't figure out how I was going to get through the next eight months!"

Right now you have only so much energy, and the baby is consuming more than its fair share. And this is in addition to your already-existing responsibilities. Before, you may have thought nothing of putting in long hours at work, freshening up, and then going out to a movie with friends. You and your mate may be used to spending your weekend pursuing athletic activities or late-night romance.

So even though you're excited about the baby, perhaps you are also feeling irritated, resentful, or downright angry about your loss of control. Although you can't do much about your reduced energy level, there are ways to cope with it.

First, you need to *learn how to say no*. During pregnancy,

your main priority is to protect yourself and your baby. This means setting limits at home and in the workplace. For now, you may need to turn down social invitations in favor of some quiet time at home. Pass up special projects and overtime hours until a later date. It can be especially difficult to say no to your employer, but it gets easier the more often you do it!

Setting limits is a valuable skill to learn for now and for later, after the baby arrives. You'll have ample opportunity to say no for the rest of your life—whether it's in response to your child's request for another cookie, or to the offer of a business trip that falls on his or her first birthday.

Another way to cope is by *asking for help.* Find out if your mate can lend a hand by making meals, running errands, or taking on more of the housework than usual. Sharing responsibilities is also an important preparation for parenthood. Once the baby comes, there will be lots more work to do than before. Now is the time to begin negotiating an equitable division of labor.

Finally, make an effort to *control yourself.* This doesn't mean censoring your feelings; instead, it means being aware of ways in which you're contributing to your own escalating stress level. Flying into a rage because your mate brought home the wrong brand of peanut butter isn't going to do either of you any good. Being short with your mother because she forgot to ask you about your doctor's appointment is unwarranted. You're certainly entitled to some mood swings, but letting your emotions run rampant will only add to your frustration.

Explore what's behind your behavior. Maybe you're working too hard to disguise your feelings of vulnerability. Maybe you need more help, reassurance, and support. Talk to your mate or your mother. A simple apology for your latest outburst may open the door for understanding and acceptance.

Taking Charge—and Letting Go

The way you cope with the loss of control has a lot to do with the kind of person you are. How do you react to other circumstances that are out of your hands? For example, what do you do when you're caught in a traffic jam? Do you lean on the horn, getting madder by the minute? Or do you roll down the window and turn on the radio, glad of the chance to have a few moments to relax?

Losing control almost invariably evokes feelings of helplessness, whether you're stuck in traffic or compelled to eat because the baby wants breakfast. There are two ways to deal with helplessness: by *taking charge,* and by *letting go.* These may sound contradictory, but, in fact, they balance each other.

TAKING CHARGE

1. *Get all the information you can.* Being informed will enable you to feel more in control. Knowing precisely what's going on inside you should help you to relax and accept the ways in which your baby is affecting your body.

   Find out how big your baby is, what it looks like, and what developmental stage it's reached. Ask your doctor, or check out a book from your local library. I found it enormously reassuring to stare at those front- and side-view line drawings showing month-by-month fetal growth. There's one terrific book that even has color photographs: *A Child Is Born* by Lennart Nilsson (revised edition, New York: Delacorte Press, 1979). Since fetuses lack hair and recognizable facial characteristics, you can assume that the one in the picture (or drawing) looks pretty much like the one inside you.

   Learn as much as possible about how your diet, sleeping patterns, and exercise are helping your baby to grow. Understanding the connection between your health and your baby's development is bound to increase your confidence and sense of security.

   Finally, talk to other pregnant women. Simply hearing them describe their physical changes and their reactions to those changes can go a long way toward helping you feel better—or at least as if you've got company.

2. *Make adjustments to your life-style.* Trying to carry on as

if nothing has changed will only add to any feelings of inadequacy you may be having. It's simply not possible, because something *has* changed: You're pregnant!

It's tough to get out of bed and arrive at work on time when the room is spinning and everything looks green. It's hard to dance all night when your feet feel as if they're made of lead. Okay—so you may be late to work a few times. Or you may decide to head home well before closing time at the nightclub. No big deal. By the time your second trimester rolls around, you may have more energy than you know what to do with; many women do. It's the first trimester that seems most taxing because of all the physical changes.

For now, reevaluate your capabilities. Be honest about what you can and can't take on, and what you can and can't continue to do.

A good way to get a handle on this is by making lists. Start by writing down the things you do in the course of a normal day. Then expand this to a week's worth of activities. Circle the ones you honestly can't do without. Draw a line through those that are less pressing. Look closely at your pared-down list. Does it seem more manageable? It should.

Take your own needs into account, and you'll be less likely to resent the baby's demands. Once the baby arrives, this process will become a way of life. You won't have the luxury of setting your priorities according to your whims. Just going out to dinner will require advance arrangements. If you plan to continue with your career, juggling that plus motherhood will involve an enormous amount of strategic planning. Learning to maximize your time and energy *now* will pave the way for the future.

3. *Do something!* Whenever I'm feeling out of control, the first thing I ask myself is, "What can I *do?*" Acknowledging your feelings, assuming responsibility for them, and doing something about them can put you back in the driver's seat.

   Feeling fatigued? Consider taking an exercise class, improving your diet, or going to bed earlier for a while. Feeling lethargic? Force yourself to go for a short walk and get some fresh air. Worried about weight gain? Buy a calorie guide and start counting.

Taking charge requires energy and determination. Both may seem in short supply, but the chances are excellent that you'll find an untapped reserve. Once you decide what to do, follow through.

Caution: don't put *too* much pressure on yourself all at once. Change takes time. It's okay to start with small steps; enough of those will get you where you want to go.

LETTING GO

Letting go can be an even greater challenge than taking charge because it means surrendering your control and accepting what's happening to you. There's an old saying that I've found helpful on more than one occasion: God grant me the courage to change what I can, the serenity to accept what I cannot change, and the wisdom to know the difference.

Maybe you just don't have the energy to climb into your leotard and go to your exercise class. Okay; skip it. Or maybe soda crackers are all you can keep down, no matter how hard you try to eat a balanced diet. Go ahead and consume your daily ration; maybe tomorrow you'll feel different.

I had the unusual experience of being terribly sick throughout both of my pregnancies. I was nauseated almost immediately upon learning that I was pregnant, and I stayed nauseated until I was on the delivery table. At first I was certain that my problem would go away once I was a little further along. I had never heard of anyone who was sick for the whole nine months; surely this couldn't happen to me!

As the days and weeks went by, it became clear that things weren't going to get any better. I tried everything: special foods, counseling, hypnosis, even acupuncture. Nothing worked, and as each new potential "cure" failed, I grew more and more depressed. I had to quit my job and cut back on almost all my activities. I was reduced to sitting on the couch, staring at the television, and praying that the air would stop moving.

I worried about how Gary and I would make it without my salary. I was angry at myself for the way I was "handling" my pregnancy. I was furious at the baby for causing so much trouble. I was frantic that it would be too small, or, God forbid, deformed because I wasn't giving it enough nourishment. I expended a great deal of energy vacillating between guilt, rage, and despair. Each day was an ordeal; nine months seemed an eternity.

I wish I could tell you that everything changed overnight. But that's not the way it happened. Instead, little by little, day by day, I gradually let go until I finally accepted the reality of my pregnancy.

I see this as a two- (maybe three-) step process. It worked for me; it may work for you.

1. *Take stock of your situation.* It became obvious to me that I couldn't do anything about my nausea. It was a fact of my pregnancy as surely as the baby was. Having always been a "take action" type of person, this was very difficult for me to face up to and accept.

   Then again, it seemed pointless to continue fighting a losing battle. Once I acknowledged this, I was able to move on to the next step.

2. *Accept yourself.* When I looked around at other pregnant women, they all seemed to be managing everything else in their lives along with the baby. They all appeared to be working and leading active social lives, while I couldn't do anything but be pregnant.

   One day I complained to a friend about the predicament I was in. "I used to be so productive," I moaned. "Now all I'm doing is growing a baby."

   Then I really *heard* what I'd just said: *All I'm doing is growing a baby*—as if creating a new life were some small, ordinary, meaningless task!

   Later that day I sat down and had a serious talk with myself. "If this is what it takes to bring a new life into the world," I said, "and if you need to quit doing everything else, then you're still doing a great deal!" Then and there, I forgave myself. Rather than feeling angry and ashamed about what I couldn't do, I began to love and appreciate myself for what I *was* doing.

3. *Draw strength from your spirituality.* People with deeply held spiritual beliefs sometimes cope more easily during difficult times; they may not have to struggle so hard to let go and accept things the way they are. Their beliefs help them understand that what's happening is happening for a reason, and that everything is part of a larger plan.

   If you're finding it tough to deal with certain areas of your pregnancy, try looking at the big picture. Your experiences may prove to be opportunities for personal growth. In coping with your sense of helplessness, for example, you may learn to be more assertive. Coming to terms with your vulnerability may increase your sensitivity toward others.

   Some of the deeper lessons of your pregnancy may not emerge until you look back on them from the distance of time. Be patient!

Letting go requires a great deal of trust, faith, and love for yourself and the incredible feat of pregnancy. No matter how your first trimester is progressing—whether you're breezing through it or coping with discomfort or illness—try to accept and celebrate yourself for carrying your child. Pregnancy is a full-time commitment. Anything else you do is extra!

HANDLING UNSOLICITED ADVICE

We all have at least one friend who's dying to tell us exactly how to act and feel during pregnancy—the implication being that we should act and feel just as *she* did. You may or may not welcome this kind of input. Maybe you've already heard enough, or you'd rather not fill your head with the suggestions that other people are so willing to give you. Support is one thing;

advice is another. It's the rare individual who can offer support without throwing in her two cents' worth.

Donna recently returned from a weekend with a friend and her two-month-old baby. "Elaine spent the entire two days nagging me," she says. "Was I aware of the terrible effects of smoking? Why had I gained so much weight? When was I going to quit working? Was I sure that six weeks of maternity leave would be enough? Now I'm wondering if worrying too much can hurt my baby. On top of everything else, I'm worrying about worrying!"

Friends can be a wonderful source of information and strength —or they can generate extra pressure on you. You'll know soon enough which of your friends fall into which category.

The same is true of your family. The advice your friends give you will pale beside the endless stream of "helpful" suggestions that come from your relatives. Some of this may take the form of family folklore. For example, maybe you've heard that your ancestors gave birth like peasants in the fields, or that none of them was ever sick for a single day.

You may find it fun and interesting to hear about how the women in your family went through pregnancy and childbirth. Or you may find it demoralizing, especially if you feel as if you're not living up to their expectations.

If your mother didn't work outside the home when she was pregnant, she may hint (or insist) that it's time for you to quit your job. If your sister kept her weight gain to twenty pounds, she may not be able to resist the urge to monitor your diet. Handling these situations will require some diplomacy on your part. Smile, nod your head, and keep doing exactly what *you* want to do!

Even casual acquaintances and strangers will get into the act. Waitresses will ask you if you've had enough to eat. People you've never seen in your life will ask you why you're carrying that heavy package all by yourself.

Betsy, eight months pregnant and the size of a U-Haul trailer, said it best: "I feel like a public building that everyone walks past and comments on!"

True, some people are sincerely trying to be nice. And it's not in the least unpleasant when they open doors for you, or offer you their seat on the bus, or stand back and let you get on the elevator first rather than shoving you out of the way. But most of the time, their comments are inappropriate, and you probably won't want to hear them.

Even little things that people say can make us cringe. Their comments may or may not be made in a spirit of caring, but somehow they feel like criticism. You don't want to appear overly sensitive or rude, but you don't want to stand there and take it, either. Simply thank them for their interest and walk away.

Most of us can easily distinguish between support and unsolicited advice. We experience support as warm and loving, while advice can sometimes make us feel angry or uncomfortable. Follow your feelings.

SORTING THROUGH WHAT YOU READ AND HEAR

Earlier we talked about taking charge and getting all the information you can. In general, the more you know, the better you'll feel about what you're going through.

Now for a word of caution: there's so *much* information out there that it can be overwhelming. A single trip to a library can turn up dozens of books and hundreds of articles on every aspect of pregnancy. Trying to take it all in is not only impossible, it can also be confusing. Many of the experts disagree with one another. And if you try to follow every piece of advice in each "how-to" article you read, you'll go crazy.

Unless you're planning to be a Professor of Pregnancy, you really don't *need* to know it all.

I spent hours staring at shelves full of books, wondering which to choose. The one with the charts, the one with the diagrams, or the one I had noticed earlier in my doctor's waiting room? Once I finally made the decision, took the book home, and sat down to read it, I faced another dilemma: How much of this was

I supposed to accept? I wanted to do *exactly* what the experts advised, but I didn't want to live in fear of making a mistake.

Choose one or two books to be friends with throughout your pregnancy. Which books you choose depends on you. Are you looking for an author who's a medical professional, someone who focuses primarily on your health and the baby's physiological development? Or are you looking for a feminist who advocates individual choice and woman-centered childbirth? Your best bet will be an author whose beliefs and values seem closest to your own. And *use your own good sense* in determining how much of what you read to take to heart. The author may know a lot about pregnancy, but he or she knows absolutely nothing about you!

If you haven't yet signed up for childbirth education classes, you may want to consider that, too. Most women find these helpful in some ways. The medical information you receive should make you feel more secure, especially during labor and delivery; transition is no time to learn about episiotomies or internal monitors. But some women don't like hearing about all the things that can go wrong. They end up fretting over possibilities that never even occurred to them. (Then again, one woman arranged to be present at a cesarean birth just in case she ever needed one. That's being informed!)

Use your judgment when deciding what to accept and what to reject. The point is to learn as much as you need to know to feel comfortable. With a solid base of knowledge to support you, you'll be able to make the kinds of decisions that are best for you and your baby.

COPING WITH YOUR FEARS

You can read everything about pregnancy that's been printed since the invention of the Gutenberg press. You can attend every childbirth education class offered within a fifty-mile radius. You can talk to your doctor every day and your mother every hour. And you can fend off other people's offhand remarks about what you should and shouldn't do.

But as hard as you try to maintain control over your pregnancy, *you'll still worry about the baby.*

You may actually find it reassuring to experience some discomfort during the first trimester. Feeling tired or slightly nauseated can be a comforting sign that there really *is* a baby in there. But until your pregnancy is showing, you can hear the baby's heartbeat, and you have passed the three-month mark, you may have a nagging fear of miscarriage.

Some women find solace in the commonly held belief that miscarriage is nature's way of responding to problems in the developing fetus. Most doctors agree that there's little anyone can do to prevent one from happening—and, if one occurs, that it's highly unlikely the woman is responsible. But time is your ally. Once you're safely in the second trimester, your fears on this point will gradually subside.

However, it may take the entire nine months to stop your worries about the possibility of birth defects. Sheila had watched her sister struggle with the hardships of raising a mentally retarded son, and she fretted constantly until her own perfectly healthy baby was born. Other women experience this as an occasional fantasy or fleeting fear.

One way to reduce your fears is by having an *ultrasound* test, if and when your medical provider agrees it's a good idea. While this test won't reveal everything about a developing fetus, it can quite accurately diagnose some serious problems.

Amniocentesis, commonly recommended for women age thirty-five and over, is a more sophisticated diagnostic tool. Unfortunately, getting the results takes about four weeks, and the wait can be agonizing. If you choose this route, you may want to consider how you will respond should the results indicate the need for a decision. You'll want to evaluate the emotional and economic factors involved in raising a special child. Your religious beliefs may lead you to favor one option over another. Imagining various scenarios in advance isn't a pleasant process, but it can prepare you to cope.

Just remember that the statistics are in your favor. Miscarriages and birth defects do happen, but far greater numbers of babies are born healthy.

CHOOSING YOUR MEDICAL PROVIDER

Until now, your involvement with doctors has probably been limited to annual checkups and occasional office visits. You make an appointment, have a fifteen-minute consultation, pick up your prescription, and go home.

Pregnancy may be the first time you'll need to enter into a significant and ongoing relationship with a member of the medical community. He or she will exercise a profound influence over your emotional experiences of both pregnancy and childbirth. That's why it's so important to choose someone who's right for you.

Fortunately, you do have a choice. Many of our mothers didn't, and they're amazed at the many options we have today. It used to be that a woman went to whatever doctor was closest; some communities only had one or two. And once she was there, she handed over all the power to him (most doctors back then were male). From that point on, he made the decisions and she did what she was told.

Those days are past. Now *you* hold the reins. There's a wide range of options available today, depending on your community.

Which would you prefer: An obstetrician-gynecologist? An M.D.? A family practitioner? A midwife? Each type of medical provider offers a unique kind of support.

The most popular choice continues to be an OB/GYN. The M.D. takes a traditional approach to medicine, which many women find comforting. A family practitioner may have a more holistic outlook; his or her knowledge of your medical history and family dynamics may offer you a more integrated experience.

More and more women are going the midwife route. Here, too, you have two options: the lay midwife, or the nurse-midwife. The former continues to be fairly controversial. Lay midwives are the subject of much folklore and are often assumed to have less medical expertise. This isn't necessarily true; it all depends on the individual. Some lay midwives have supervised at more births than many doctors. And many are widely respected for the intimate care and nurturing they bring to the job.

Nurse-midwives are trained in traditional medicine and usually work in cooperation with an OB/GYN. A nurse-midwife offers one way to combine your desire for the latest in medical technology and a hospital birth with a greater degree of personal involvement.

Each of these choices has its advantages and disadvantages. The best approach is to carefully select a medical provider who will offer the kind of support and care *you* want—and spend plenty of time doing it.

If you were about to hire a secretary, you'd go through an exhaustive process of interviewing candidates and thoroughly checking references. You should do the same when selecting your medical provider. Neither hearsay, convenience, nor habit should be good enough for you and your baby. Make your decision carefully and consciously.

Here's a tried-and-true way to approach it:

1. For *each* medical provider you're considering, start by making an appointment for an interview. Be sure to let the receptionist know the nature of your visit, and request at least a half-hour appointment. Find out beforehand whether you'll be charged and, if so, how much.
2. Be prepared to ask detailed questions. Start with these and add your own.
   - How often will I need to come in for appointments?
   - How long does each appointment typically last? What if I need more time?
   - What are your attitudes concerning diet and exercise during pregnancy?
   - How do you feel about pregnant women taking medications? What about medications during birth?
   - On average, how much time do patients spend in your waiting room?
   - Will my mate be welcome at my prenatal visits? What should his role be during the birth?
   - Is there anyone else in your practice who may be involved in my prenatal care? Who will attend my baby's birth in the event that you're not available?

- Do you allow other people to be present at the birth? Why or why not? If so, who?
- What do you consider to be the "ideal" birth experience? What's your concept of a "difficult" birth?
- How much do you charge? What is your payment schedule? What kinds of insurance coverage do you accept?

Bring your questions *in writing* so you won't run the risk of forgetting any of them. And remember: *you're* in charge of this situation.

Your ultimate decision will rest on a combination of factors, including the medical provider's credentials and experience. But there's another, less concrete aspect you should consider: his or her personal style.

What kind of person are *you* most comfortable with: someone formal, or someone who's relaxed and easygoing? Would you prefer a down-to-business type or one who likes to chat? Are a white coat and a stethoscope important to you, or would you rather meet with someone in jeans? Do you care if your medical provider has a sense of humor? And—this is more important than you may think—how will you address each other? If your doctor wants to be known as Dr. So-and-so and not as Bob or Sue, then you have the right to be called Mrs. or Ms. or Miss. Whatever form of address applies, it ought to be used by both parties.

The power of choice isn't the only power you have. Once you've settled on a medical provider, you still have a lot of say over what happens from then on. You're entering a relationship, not a dictatorship. Keep asking questions. Talk openly about your wishes and needs. You've invited this person to participate in your pregnancy, not the other way around. And if things don't work out the way you want them to, you can always find someone else.

FOR SINGLE MOTHERS-TO-BE

Going through pregnancy as a couple is a challenge; going through it as a single person is even more difficult. It doesn't matter that millions of women before you have done what you're doing. You're still a pioneer.

How you feel at the moment is probably closely connected to the circumstances surrounding your pregnancy. Too many women never intended to end up pregnant and on their own. If this describes you, you're to be congratulated for choosing to continue. It couldn't have been easy.

On the other hand, more and more women today are opting to have babies because they want them, regardless of whether there's a mate in the picture full-time. This also merits congratulations. Raising a child is a big job for two people; it's twice as big for one.

But there are real advantages to this approach, too. You don't have to worry about being a perfect pregnant wife or girlfriend. You don't have to answer to anyone else. You can make decisions without taking a vote. Your pregnancy is your own; your baby will belong only to you.

Still, you're going to need some kind of support system. The formal and informal networks available to women with mates may not be open to you. You may feel like an outsider in your childbirth classes. You may not enjoy the casual camaraderie available to pregnant women who are halves of a team.

Many single mothers-to-be (and single mothers) create a support system of concerned friends and family members. You'll want a close friend to talk to, a sister to share with, or another trusted person to be with you during the birth. If possible, start developing relationships now with other single pregnant women. Because they've made the same choice you have, they'll be more likely to understand your needs.

You're apt to be especially vulnerable to other people's perceptions and judgments. You may find yourself constantly fielding questions and reassuring people that you're doing what's right for you.

You may also have to defend your decision to have a baby alone. Most of us have been taught to believe that children are the sole property of married women, even though this isn't true. People may express their concern about your ability to support your child, the lack of an at-home father figure, or even your right to conceive. Some of them will speak out of genuine caring for you, while others will be motivated by prejudice or narrow-mindedness. You'll usually be able to tell the difference and react accordingly. The caring ones may be worth bringing into your support system; the others you may choose to educate or avoid.

As anyone who has ever followed a nontraditional path discovers, the key to success rests with your own courage and confidence. If you know in your heart that a baby is exactly what you want, you'll be better equipped to deal with other people's expectations.

Meanwhile, there are many places you can turn to for information and support. Here are just a few.[1]

Stephen Atlas, *Single Parenting: A Practical Resource Guide* (Englewood Cliffs, N.J.: Prentice-Hall, 1981)

Parents Without Partners Information Center
7910 Woodmont Avenue
Bethesda, Maryland 20014

Single Parent Resource Center
3896 24th Street
San Francisco, California 94114

Robert Weiss, *Going It Alone: The Family Life and Social Situation of the Single Parent* (New York: Basic Books, 1979)

Stage Two

5

THIRTEEN WEEKS:
You Made It!

If you've reached your thirteenth week of pregnancy, go ahead and breathe a sigh of relief. The chance that you'll have a miscarriage has just dropped dramatically to less than 2 percent.

For many women, this out-of-the-woods stage signals the beginning of full-fledged, "official" pregnancy. Not only are you almost certain to reach term, you may also be starting to show. Forget about having to tell people to whom you haven't yet broken the news. They'll see for themselves soon enough.

Go ahead and sign up for childbirth education classes, if you haven't already. If you're in the mood, begin shopping for maternity clothes (more about that later). It's okay to strut a little, too! In fact, this may be the first time in over three months that you've felt capable of strutting (or even of staying awake past eight in the evening).

HOW ARE YOU FEELING, DEAR?

Right about now, people are probably starting to ask you that question—at work, over lunch, in the elevator. And you may be ready to answer, "Terrific, thanks!"

You're likely experiencing a combination of anticipation and exhilaration. You have so much to look forward to, and you finally have the energy to enjoy it. And if you still have doubts, they'll soon be put to rest—the first time you hear your baby's heartbeat or feel the first kick.

These are wondrous, magical moments: listening to that otherworldly whooshing of the fetuscope, sensing the faint flutters of movement. They affirm your pregnancy more than all the books and doctors in the world ever could.

Most of the discomforts of early pregnancy should have passed. In most cases, any nausea you suffered will have disappeared (or waned), and you should need less sleep than you used to. Don't take these as absolutes, however; "should" doesn't mean "must," and there isn't anything wrong with you if you're still running for the bathroom in the mornings or nodding over your desk in the afternoons. You'll probably feel better soon.

Women often say that starting the second trimester is like waking from a deep sleep. They're relaxed, refreshed, and raring to go.

Perhaps you're suddenly realizing that you haven't been out at night with your mate for a while. Or maybe you're noticing that your plants have turned pale with neglect. You may start exercising regularly, cleaning house like a whirlwind, or barreling in to work in a storm of energy. You're feeling like your old self again, with the extra punch that pregnancy provides.

Going to your monthly checkups adds to your enthusiasm. Most women look forward to these progress reports and to the professional support of a medical provider. Just being there reinforces your identity as a pregnant woman. Some of the most pleasurable moments of my pregnancies took place in my doctor's waiting room; one of the other mothers-to-be would initiate a conversation, and soon we'd all be comparing notes on due dates, weight gain, and where to shop for maternity clothes. These informal rap sessions were *fun*. Besides, there's nothing quite like talking to other pregnant women. They know exactly what you're going through, and they have generous supplies of empathy and encouragement to share with you.

Regardless of whether you're showing, it should be getting easier to discuss your pregnancy with others. You're in possession of more concrete information, and you're more confident about your baby's well-being. The fact that you're going to have a baby is joyful news, and most people will be interested and delighted to hear it. Bask in the attention as you become more secure in your new and emerging identity.

You may also be experiencing a sensation of added weight or heaviness. This doesn't refer only to pounds (although you are surely putting on a few of those), but also to the seriousness of the situation you're in. Your relief at being over the hump may well be accompanied by apprehension, surprise, and a gradual awareness of the *permanence* of the change you're undergoing.

Being pregnant is one thing; having a baby is another, and you're getting closer every minute. We're talking *serious stuff* here: diapers, swing sets, report cards, and graduation parties, not to mention the estimated $85,000 or more it takes to raise a child to age twenty-one. One of these days, all this is going to hit you over the head (if it hasn't already). Or maybe it will creep up on you little by little and you'll find yourself staring at other women's babies and clipping coupons for wet-wipes.

Pregnancy is a passage from one world into another. Picture it as a long hall between two doors, an old familiar one you've left behind and a brand-new one ahead. The old one is closed to you forever. But the new one looks inviting: There's light shining out all around it.

HOW YOU SEE YOURSELF

Once the reality of what you're doing sinks in, you'll want to start taking stock of your life. You may already be seeing yourself through different eyes. Sometimes you'll feel as if you're wearing rose-colored glasses; at other times, your vision will seem distorted and out of focus.

Your identity is rapidly evolving, and you're not yet sure what the outcome will be. Thirteen short weeks ago, before you were pregnant, you knew who you were and what mattered to you. You chose your mate, your friends, your activities, and your career based on those certainties. Your life-style reflected your personal priorities and goals.

Knowing that you're going to be a mother forces you to reevaluate your relationships, your life-style, your politics, and your spiritual beliefs. It compels you to look closely at who you were, who you are, and who you're about to be.

Maybe your decision to get pregnant was a deliberate attempt to change yourself, to add another dimension to the woman you saw in the mirror every morning.

Here's an interesting experiment you may want to try. Find a fairly recent photograph of yourself—you alone, minus mate or the family dog. Now imagine adding a baby to that picture. (If you need help, cut a photo of a baby out of a magazine and use it to bolster your imagination.) What do you see? Does the baby make *you* look any different? More responsible? More mature? Terrified?

"Terrified" was what Denise came up with. "I'm afraid that once my baby is born, I'll go shopping and forget it under a pile of clothes in the fitting room." What she's *really* voicing is a fear that she isn't responsible enough to be a good mother.

Motherhood will cause you to call upon whatever qualities you have, apparent or hidden. You may find yourself using talents, skills, and sensibilities you didn't realize you possessed. And you may discover the need to develop others. Patience, a sense of humor, and the ability to discipline calmly and lovingly are among those you'll want to have on hand in your future as a parent. Take time now to find out what you like about yourself and where you could stand some improvement.

If it's hard to be objective about yourself, ask someone else to describe your strengths and weaknesses. Mates and best friends are especially good sources of honest feedback!

Over the next several months, you'll not only be growing a whole new person, you'll also be growing *into* a whole new person. As you watch yourself change, you'll see traces of who you were and hints of who you're becoming.

HOW YOU SEE YOUR MATE

You'll also start seeing your mate in another light entirely: the light of prospective fatherhood. What kind of dad will he be? Will he cheerfully change a diaper at four A.M. (someone has to do it!), or will he complain or leave it for you? More to the point, how will he get you to the hospital on time when he's always late to dinner?

Guess what: he's probably asking himself similar questions about you. He may not be saying much, but you can bet that he's wondering—about what kind of mom you'll be, whether you'll want him to help with the baby, how motherhood will change you and your relationship with him.

At the moment, you may *both* be examining each other sideways. Come right out with it: *Ask* each other the questions you're thinking about. This may enhance your mutual appreciation; it may even bring about a renaissance of your partnership. Of course, it may also reveal some serious conflicts or doubts.

However compatible the two of you are, you're not going to have identical notions of what a child will mean to your life together. You may be anticipating staying home with the baby; he may be counting on you going back to work and contributing a paycheck to the family coffers. He may believe that the size of your home is adequate; you may be hoping for an addition with a nursery. He's worried about your lack of neatness; you're concerned about his lack of patience. Don't let this escalate into you're-a-slob, he's-a-hothead. None of this is cause for divorce!

Pregnancy is a perfect opportunity for the two of you to build and cement your relationship. Many of these issues probably would have arisen sooner or later. Having a baby merely speeds the process. Still, you may both find it difficult to express your feelings—especially the negative ones. Women have been taught not to make waves; men have learned that it's somehow unmanly to talk about things that are bothering them.

Even if the two of you have what you consider an ideal marriage, you're probably both experiencing some deep-seated anxieties. For a woman, the worst is usually the fear of being left alone as a single mother. Pregnancy may increase your feelings of dependency as you become more aware of the emotional and economic support you need from your mate.

Speak up! Express your positive *and* negative feelings about each other and your relationship. If doing this extemporaneously is hard for you, use the incomplete statements that follow as a starting point. Sit down together some evening (or stay in bed late some Saturday morning), read them aloud, and fill in the blanks with whatever pops into your head. Then have your mate do the same.

1. Having a baby is going to be _____.
2. When the baby comes, we'll both need to _____.
3. I know I'll be a good parent because I'm _____, _____, and _____.
4. I'd be a better parent if I could just _____and _____.
5. I want to have a baby with you because you're _____, _____, and _____.
6. I know you'll be a good parent because you're _____, _____, and _____.
7. I worry sometimes about your tendency to _____.
8. Having a baby together will make our relationship more _____.

Pay attention to the similarities and differences in your answers. Is there something you need to talk about in greater detail? Is there anything that either of you found surprising? What made you happy? What made you unhappy or angry?

You may want to repeat this exercise at a later point in your pregnancy. It can be a useful tool for keeping the lines of communication open between you.

DOLLARS AND SENSE

Taking stock also means looking long and hard at your financial situation. Those wonderful, cuddly, cute little creatures known as babies cost a *lot* of money.

Right now your baby has a cozy, climate-controlled room of its own. How will you provide for it when its lease runs out? Will you be a two-career, two-income family? If not, which of you will stay home? Is day care an affordable option?

Maybe you've been saving for years in anticipation of your pregnancy—squirreling away dimes and dollars and investing wisely. Or maybe you're scrimping and sweating over how far you can realistically expect your budget to stretch. Or maybe you're entering sweepstakes every week in hopes of striking it rich.

For most of us, money is an emotionally loaded subject. It symbolizes security, and our attitudes toward money are a clue to our values. How much is enough? That depends on whom you talk to. What looks like a fortune to one person may seem like a pittance to another.

I've known parents who have parked cribs in hallways. I've also seen nurseries with solid-brass cradles and designer wallpaper. To the best of my knowledge, the babies didn't sleep any differently.

If you and your spouse haven't yet talked about how having a child is going to affect your financial situation, *do it soon*. It may not be an issue at the moment, but it will be. Guaranteed.

Brand-new clothes or hand-me-downs, expensive toys or milk-carton castles, private schools or public education—all these are economic decisions, not just philosophical ones. The choices you make will reflect both your beliefs and your financial circumstances.

For example, you might start thinking about how often you plan to use baby-sitters. The going rate in many neighborhoods is $2 an hour. In large cities it can be as much as $5 an hour. When an evening starts at seven and ends at midnight, that adds up. On the other hand, you must have time for yourselves, so it will sometimes be worth it. There are parents who use sitters every week, parents who rarely use sitters, and others who never do; they don't like to leave their children, or they'd rather spend their money on other things. It's a matter of convictions and priorities.

Money can be a very touchy subject, and the baby-sitter decision is only the tip of the iceberg. Before you can spend money on anything, it has to be there for the spending. What this means for most of us is that someone has to earn it. And this leads to the broad and complex issue of whether to work outside the home once the baby is born.

To Work, or Not to Work?

This may not be an issue because you may not have a choice. The dad-at-the-office, mom-at-home-with-2.5-kids myth is just that: a myth. The so-called average American family is really the exception. Some 65 percent of American mothers between the ages of eighteen and forty are in the work force; some 18 percent are heads of households (read: single parents).[1] Few women today have the luxury of deciding whether to work, and those who do are very fortunate indeed.

But all the statistics in the world don't make it any easier on the individual level. We're talking about *your* baby. Who's going to care for it after it's born? Naturally you believe that nobody is better qualified for this job than you. And, let's face it, keeping a one-year-old safe and stimulated for ten hours at a stretch *is* a job. *Every* mother is a working mother!

Whatever you do—keep your job or stay at home—will have numerous emotional and economic repercussions. This is especially true for the single mom who bears all the burdens alone. If this describes you, you may already have some idea of what's in store. Not only will you be the only breadwinner, you'll be the only parent. You'll have to depend heavily on quality child care. You'll have fewer backups when something goes awry.

Most young couples today can't get along without two incomes. But that doesn't make the decision to leave a child easy to accept. Perhaps you always envisioned yourself staying home with your baby; most of our mothers quit their jobs when we were born. You may feel frustrated or angry about having to continue working, especially if you really don't want to. The everyday demands of your job may seem like intrusions or obstacles to your relationship with your child. And you may worry that you'll lose your enthusiasm for the nine-to-five routine.

Let's assume for a moment that both you and your spouse will continue working outside the home, whether out of necessity or choice. Just because this decision has been made doesn't mean that the heat is off. Who will stay home when the baby gets sick? (The baby *will get sick*. Fevers, ear infections, croup, sore throats, the flu—we could fill pages of this book describing ailments that are common to infants.) Who will stay up all night when the baby can't sleep? Who will be on call for emergencies?

These things should be settled *before* the baby arrives. What it may take is an honest evaluation of both careers—yours and your spouse's. Because something, somewhere, is going to have to give.

Unless you make other arrangements, one of you will have to leave work when the baby-sitter or day-care center telephones to report that your baby is ill. One of you will have to take your baby to the doctor for regular checkups and shots. And so on, ad infinitum. Rather than have this be a constant source of conflict for the next eighteen years, do your best to make some decisions *now*.

It may help to start by asking questions like these:

1. Who makes more money? (In other words, whose income could you absolutely *not* do without?)
2. Who has the more flexible job, in terms of being able to take time off or leave the office at a moment's notice?
3. Whose place of employment seems to be more liberal and understanding of parents' needs and responsibilities? (Find out about co-workers' experiences.)

4. Who would suffer the harsher penalties (docked pay, or maybe even the loss of a job) if push came to shove?
5. Who is on a "career track" that can't be interrupted without jeopardizing it?

Try to look forward in time—to six months after the baby is born, two years after, five years after, ten years after. Try *not* to let the discussion disintegrate into an argument. "I'm a man—my job is more important!" and "Haven't you heard? Women are supposed to be equal!" are the kinds of statements that won't get you anywhere. In fact, if at all possible, each of you should imagine yourself on the outside looking in, with lots of objectivity.

There's another question that needs to be answered: Once you pay for child care, will you still come out ahead? We're talking anywhere from $70 to $250 per week for an infant, depending on what part of the country you live in and what kind of care you get. (At the low end are day-care providers who work out of their homes; at the high end are live-in nannies.) What's it worth to you?

Even if you're able to afford day care, you'll still have to come to terms with balancing your needs and the baby's. How will you cope with someone else mothering your child, even if it's only from nine to five? How important is your job to your sense of self-esteem? Your feelings may change after your baby is born. Are you prepared to reconsider them?

Barbara has her mind made up. She's planning to work from her home until her baby is six weeks old and then return full-time to her job. She's been the assistant manager of a leasing company for five years, and she loves the challenge and status of her position. Needless to say, the money doesn't hurt, either.

"I'd go crazy if I didn't work," she says. "I can't imagine staying home all day, changing diapers and singing nursery rhymes. Anyway, I believe in quality, not quantity. If I'm happy with what I'm doing, I'll be a better mother. And I'll be in a much better position to give the baby the material things it needs."

It should be this easy for all of us, but it isn't. Let's turn this issue around and look at it from the other side.

What if you decide to stay home with your baby? Will you have to make financial sacrifices? Serious financial sacrifices? I'm not talking here about holding on to the BMW for an extra year before trading it in for a new one; I'm talking about *never* having enough money for a movie or a night out. Are you and your mate willing to make major life-style changes?

How about changes in the roles you both play? If you're at home all day, chances are you'll end up assuming most of the household duties as well as the child care ones. Your mate may expect dinner to be on the table when he comes through the door at night. How will you handle situations like these?

And once you stop earning an income, will you have less say in how money is spent around your house? If so, is that an even trade for those months and years you'll have with your baby, watching it grow?

Joyce is the mother of three children: an infant, a toddler, and a demanding three-year-old. She takes care of them twenty-four hours a day, seven days a week. Her husband is a sales rep who travels during the week and is often on the road for several weeks at a time. Before she had children, Joyce worked as a nurse. When asked if she ever misses her old job, she says, "No, but I sure miss the money! I'm always having to ask Eric for money, even if it's just for groceries. It would be awfully nice to have some of my own."

Joyce works as hard as anyone with an outside job. It would cost an arm and a leg to pay someone to do what she does. Yet she has to *ask* her husband for money, and it's obvious that she doesn't feel good about it.

If at all possible, avoid getting yourself into this position. Once again, the best time to work things out is *before* the baby arrives. If you're going to be responsible for grocery shopping, buying baby things, and handling other household expenses, then a portion of your mate's income should regularly go to you.

How large a portion? That depends on the size of the income, your household budget, and various other factors. You may decide on an amount now and have to revise it later, so it's best to be flexible. But *do* decide on *something*. It's important to your self-esteem.

Speaking of self-esteem, what's going to happen to it when you stop working outside the home? How will this affect your sense of identity? Will you resent the baby for "interrupting" your career? Will you miss your co-workers and the camaraderie you have on the job? This is no small step you're taking. Be prepared!

Look around your neighborhood for other women who've made the same choice you're about to make. Like the woman down the street—the one you've been ignoring because "all she does is stay home with her kids." Who knows? Maybe she used to be a stockbroker, or a teacher, or a computer programmer, or vice-president of a bank. Maybe she can help you with what you're going through.

The point is, *neither* choice is easy. Each exacts definite costs —in money, in emotions, in your sense of self, and in your relationships with others, including your mate. *The only right choice is the one that's right for you.*

Not long after Zoe was born, I went to hear a psychologist speak about the personal struggles of career mothers versus stay-at-home mothers. I was then working a full-time job: rushing out of the house by eight A.M. and back in at six P.M. with my head spinning and my feet aching. I never had a moment to clear the clutter from my head, and I always felt the pressure of making up for lost time with my child.

The psychologist said something very simple, yet very reassuring: "Mothers with careers feel guilty because they spend so much time away from their children. Mothers who stay home full-time worry that their children aren't getting enough outside stimulation." In other words, no matter what you decide, you're going to have to live with a little guilt. The important thing is to be honest about what *you* want and need.

Whether having a career is a necessity or an option, you'll have to spend time away from your child. And you'll have to accept this as fact, without letting it eat away at you. The payoff will be your ability to give your child other gifts—financially, and as an alternative role model.

If you choose to stay at home, you may miss the stimulation

of a career, and you may have to forego some monetary luxuries. But you'll be able to give your child more time and attention.

Either approach represents tradeoffs; neither decision has to be permanent. When my first child was a baby, I enjoyed my career but missed seeing her take her first step. When my second one was born, I found a way to work from home so I could more easily combine motherhood with my career. In each case, I managed to be happy with the way things were.

Make arrangements that will best suit *your* personal needs and goals.

LIFE-STYLE—AND SUBSTANCE

Your life-style comprises more than the amount of money you have to spend and what you spend it on. It also includes your social, community, and spiritual involvements. Is your life-style a true reflection of the person you're becoming? Or is it time to make choices in this area, too?

Some of your friends may no longer be meeting your needs for closeness and companionship. Sometimes these will be the friends who don't have children. Don't blame them if they can't relate to your new interests and concerns. (Think back to before you were pregnant, or before you knew you wanted to be; you were probably bored by discussions of car seats, pediatricians, and the relative virtues of breast- versus bottle-feeding.)

You can do one of two things: Try to bring them along on your journey, or gracefully let them go. Don't assume that people without children won't be interested in yours. Some may delight in assuming the role of "aunt" or "uncle" to your child and perceive this as strengthening and deepening their friendship with you.

Be open to new relationships. People you never thought you had anything in common with may suddenly seem interesting. Good places for making new contacts include childbirth education classes and your medical provider's waiting room.

You'll become more aware of friends who do have children. You're probably bursting with questions, and they may well be willing to share their insights and experiences with you. (Think back again, this time to friends you may have grown apart from when *they* started having kids. Consider renewing your acquaintance.)

CAUTION: Although your baby may be at the center of your life, keep some other interests active. *Nobody* wants to talk about kids *all* the time. Even *you* will get tired of the subject, sooner or later.

Jennifer moved from New York to Minneapolis when she realized that none of her friends there had kids and they probably never would. She and her husband decided to put down roots in a new community, where they could develop enduring relationships with other young families.

You shouldn't have to move halfway across the country, but you should take a close look at where you live now. Is the neighborhood safe for children? Are there other children around? What kinds of day care are available in your area? How is the school system? Are there parks, museums, and playgrounds nearby?

What about religion? Will you want to give your child a religious education? Formal or informal? If you don't now belong to an organized place of worship, being a parent may increase your desire to join one. Or you may feel perfectly capable of passing on your spiritual values without anyone else's help.

Kate, who hadn't been to church for years, started going again when her son was born. "We live in a Judeo-Christian culture," she explains, "and I consider Sunday school a necessary part of his education. Later on, he can make up his own mind, but at least it will be an informed choice."

These are just some of the issues you'll be facing over the next months and years, and now is a good time to start thinking about them. As your pregnancy continues, you'll probably keep scrutinizing your life-style. And you'll start making changes to accommodate your new life with your child.

INVESTING YOURSELF IN YOUR PREGNANCY

Taking stock seems like such a practical process—examining your relationships, balancing your checkbook, researching day care. In truth, though, it requires a great deal of soul-searching and self-examination.

You may experience some feelings of sadness as you move through the passages of pregnancy. You're growing out of one stage of your life and into another, and this means saying good-bye to much of what's comfortable and familiar.

Nine months . . . 40 weeks . . . 282 days . . . 6,768 hours . . . Pregnancy takes a long time, yet it may seem as if it's going by in a blinding rush. Part of this is due to the fact that it brings so many changes. You're just getting used to one part of it, and you're immediately faced with a new set of challenges. Each requires emotional adjustments.

For some women, pregnancy feels like a state of limbo, a time when they're hanging in mid-air with their feet dangling above the ground. Or they may feel as if they're on a roller coaster, careening madly down one incline after another.

It's certainly one of the least appreciated (and most quickly forgotten) experiences of our lives. Too often we dismiss it as a means to an end: Once we have the baby, our mission is accomplished.

But are we being fair to ourselves? Granted, pregnancy is a temporary condition, but it's hardly an insignificant one. It deserves more attention than most people give it. Imagine yourself moving into an apartment with a nine-month lease. Do you hang up the curtains and meet the neighbors, or do you live out of boxes until it's time to move on?

You'll get more out of your pregnancy if you put more into it —more of *yourself*. Treating it as business-as-usual will prevent you from fully appreciating the changes you're going through and how important they are. Instead, live in it. Take the time and make the effort to experience and understand your body and your feelings.

It won't be long before your pregnancy is over. You'll never have another one like it. Once the baby comes, your life will be changed forever. *Now* is the time to move into your pregnancy. Make a commitment to it, devote your energy to it, invest yourself in it 100 percent. You'll be glad you did.

FOR OVER-35 MOTHERS-TO-BE

You're no longer a glaring exception to the rule. Many women your age are opting to have babies and feeling secure in their decision. You should, too. So what if you're not twenty-two anymore? In many ways, you're better off.

For one, you're probably better prepared for a baby than most younger women are. More than likely you underwent an intense process of deliberation before getting pregnant. You may have looked carefully at everything from your income to the decor of your home.

Your relationships are more settled, your career is further along, your life-style is better established, your finances are more secure, and your beliefs are more firmly embedded. So you're in *great* shape to be a mom.

You're also somewhat set in your ways. This has its good points—and its not-so-good ones. Change is the essence of pregnancy. Somewhere along the line, you're going to have to accommodate motherhood by making adjustments.

If you've been free to come and go at will for the past fifteen years, you'll need to bend a little once the baby arrives. Sitters and schedules will complicate things. The appearance of your home will alter as you put plastic plugs in electrical outlets, gates in front of stairways, and covers on doorknobs. Childproofing can be a decorator's nightmare.

One the other hand, you've never been more ready to welcome a baby into your life. You have a clearer understanding of yourself and a more evolved view of the world. You've already accomplished some of your goals, and you'll be able to give your child the benefit of your years of wisdom and experience.

Modern medicine has made mid-life pregnancies far safer than they used to be. Still, you may need to have amniocentesis (if you haven't already); many doctors recommend it for women thirty-five and over. It involves taking a sample of amniotic fluid and subjecting it to a series of tests. The results of those tests can indicate any chromosomal abnormalities. They can also tell you the sex of the child you're carrying, if you want to know (many women don't). Talk about being prepared!

6

GETTING WHAT YOU NEED

It was very still and quiet in the house. I glanced at the clock near the bed: two A.M. The baby had begun its nightly tumbling act. I looked over at Gary sleeping peacefully beside me, unaware of the silent dance taking place within my body.

A sudden awareness flooded through me: *I alone* was carrying our baby. We had conceived it together, but *I was responsible for its life*.

A series of "what ifs" clicked through my mind. What if something happened to Gary and I had to go through this alone? What if my nausea *never* went away? What if my body never got back in shape? What if I couldn't find good day care? What if my doctor was away on vacation when I went into labor? What if, what if, what if?

That was the moment I realized how much my life had changed.

Before I was pregnant, I had prided myself on being strong and independent. Now I had serious concerns about whether I could handle the many decisions I was responsible for. With another life to consider, I was intensely aware of my need for support.

"Need" is a word with certain connotations; it makes us think of poverty, sickness, and other serious problems. In recent years, it has also come to symbolize weakness, and that's unfortunate. The ability to express needs ought to be perceived as a sign of strength.

There's a difference between neediness and having needs, just as there's a difference between dependency and being able to depend on someone. Neediness and dependency are symptomatic of unhealthy relationships. Being aware of your needs and being able to depend on others are components of an emotionally sound life. When you tell someone, "I need your help," this means that you realize your limitations and are confident enough to ask for assistance. When you say, "I need to be loved," you're showing emotional honesty and courage.

GETTING IN TOUCH WITH YOUR NEEDS

The changes occurring during your pregnancy are affecting both your physical and emotional needs. The physical ones are most obvious. Many women feel a greater need for physical support. After operating for years at a familiar level of physical ease and stamina, it can be disconcerting suddenly to feel off balance, drop things, and bump into furniture. Then again, other women feel great. They're on an "estrogen high" from the moment of conception, filled with energy and more active than ever.

How does *your* body feel? Are you growing into your pregnancy comfortably, or does it seem as if your brain has been transplanted into the body of a stranger?

There may be times when the physical changes you're experiencing prove overwhelming. Here are some basic coping tips.

- Give yourself lots of room, literally and figuratively. Move the seat back in the car. Don't try to squeeze into too-tight clothes. Be patient with yourself, even if you feel like a big clumsy oaf. (You're not a big clumsy oaf, you're a beautiful pregnant woman.)

- Keep your sense of humor intact. This doesn't mean that you should balance ashtrays on your belly during cocktail parties and wait for the baby to kick them off. But there will be occasions when you look pretty funny, even if that isn't your intention. Be willing to laugh at yourself.
- If you need help, *ask for it*. I know how difficult this can be, but try!
- If someone offers help, don't bristle—*take it*. Sometimes you'll need a hand, whether it's with cooking, cleaning, or getting out of bed in the morning. If you're lucky enough to have people around you who are willing and able, enjoy!

Naturally you don't want people to think you're different simply because you're pregnant. But the fact is, you *are* different. The physical changes of pregnancy have altered your energy, your strength, and your ability to get things done. This is nothing to be ashamed of.

Your emotional needs are more complex and may be less obvious—although the signs may be very apparent. Since when does losing your keys make you fly into a rage? Have you threatened to run away from home in the middle of an argument with your mate? Does deciding what to make for dinner leave you in a puddle of tears?

What's going on? Why have you suddenly switched from being a sane and reasonable person to a hysterical, shrieking, weeping female? Relax: You haven't. You're still a normal pregnant woman.

Admittedly, you may feel out of kilter one moment and quite calm the next. Some days you're in the pits, others you're on top of the world. There are reasons for these kaleidoscopic feelings.

Hormonal changes can and do affect our emotions, but they're not the *only* cause of your ups and downs. Like the old line, Oh, she's just cranky because she's got her period, it's sexist and insulting to assume that your emotions are mere products of your female organs. When a pregnant woman bursts into tears because her shoelace broke, those tears reflect deeper feelings of sadness, fear, and confusion.

Don't dismiss your emotions as silly "female" symptoms, and don't let others do it, either. Respect them, stay in touch with them, talk about them, heed them. They're trying to tell you something. Maybe you need some time alone. Maybe you need some affection. Maybe you need a good laugh. (Maybe you need a piece of chocolate fudge—just this once.)

YOUR NEEDS AND YOUR RELATIONSHIPS

The emotional ups and downs of pregnancy can also affect your relationships. Whether you're dealing with your mate, your mother, your doctor, or your boss, you may feel less confident than you used to.

You and your mate need more from each other right now— more emotional support, more reassurance, more tenderness and affection. You need more from your medical provider—information, advice, and guidance, as well as support and encouragement. And you need greater understanding from your boss and your co-workers.

Your emerging identity as a mother is competing with your roles as wife, daughter, and career woman. The latter may have the greatest potential for conflict. Your concentration may be affected as you're distracted by thoughts of the baby. Perhaps two 15-minute breaks and a 45-minute lunch hour aren't sufficient any more. Maybe you can no longer handle the physically demanding parts of your job, such as lifting, carrying, and moving equipment. And if you plan to continue working after the baby comes, you should start negotiating your maternity leave— a formal process of stating your needs and getting them met.

But what you need most from everyone you deal with is *acceptance for who you are becoming.* At some point, the people in your life will have to acknowledge that you're a new person with a new set of feelings and needs. You can help them by *accepting yourself.*

Part of this process involves accepting your needs. Many of us have a tough time with this. Women in particular have been taught to push down anything other than "nice" feelings. We've been trained to be "good little girls"—polite, clean creatures who put up and shut up. Nobody ever taught us that it's okay to be assertive about our needs.

Unfortunately, unmet needs don't fade away. They fester and boil beneath the surface.

Maggie wishes that her husband were more involved in her pregnancy. He refuses to go along on her OB appointments, to touch her belly, or even to talk about the baby. She feels isolated and afraid.

Betsy's mother keeps saying, "Gee, I only gained fifteen pounds with you!" Every time she does, Betsy feels tight and resentful inside.

Carol always returns from the doctor with a list of unanswered questions. She feels frustrated and angry.

Mimi's boss is constantly cracking jokes about how she's ruining her career by having a baby. She knows he's just kidding, but something about his humor doesn't feel right.

Speaking up may or may not help these women; saying nothing certainly won't.

If there ever was a good time to start expressing your feelings, this is it. And try not to judge yourself by your prepregnancy standards. If you can no longer carry a forty-pound bag of groceries up three flights of stairs, it's not because you're weak or lazy. If you'd rather watch television than discuss philosophy, you're not turning into a couch potato.

I was very aware of needing more support during pregnancy, but whenever I asked Gary to bring me something, I apologized when I should have said thank you. He didn't seem to mind doing things for me, but I minded asking.

It was even more difficult being pregnant in the outside world. I didn't want pregnancy to tarnish my image as a "together person," especially at work. I was determined not to be treated any differently. No wonder my co-workers weren't sensitive to my needs (although they were excited about the baby); I never let them show. If I had it to do over, I'd wear a sign saying, The baby is fine. What about me?

Most women feel torn between wanting their needs to be noticed and not wanting anyone to make a big deal over them being pregnant. There *are* some risks involved in asserting your needs: You sacrifice some of your independence and become more vulnerable.

On the other hand, it's important to be able to *take* for a change. Letting other people nurture you is one of the things you get to enjoy when you're pregnant. Take advantage of it while it lasts!

SURE STEPS TO MEETING YOUR NEEDS

Any large task becomes easier when you break it down into smaller steps and tackle each one individually. This enables you to see your progress and determine whether you're accomplishing what you set out to do.

Getting your needs met is a fairly involved process, so you may find it helpful to break it down into these four steps:

1. identifying your feelings
2. defining your needs
3. creating solutions
4. asking for support

Identifying Your Feelings

It isn't always easy to know what we're feeling or to put a name to it. You've probably had the experience of feeling slightly anxious or down in the dumps, but when someone asks you what's wrong, you can't put your finger on the problem.

Examining your feelings is *not* a self-indulgent waste of time. In fact, it's a healthy part of being a whole person. If you don't know what you're feeling and why, you can't begin to get what you need.

Somewhere along the line, someone has probably told you, "Don't take yourself so seriously!" But if you don't, who will? You're the only one who can look inside and find out what's bothering you. Giving the problem a name is the first step toward doing something about it.

Defining Your Needs

What would it take to make you feel better? Figuring that out is a critical step, because it keeps you from getting stuck in your feelings.

For example: you think you're fat and ugly, and that makes you feel bad. Maybe you're not getting enough exercise. Maybe an improper diet is causing extra weight gain or bloatedness. Maybe you're trying to squeeze into clothes that should be moved to the back of your closet for now. Or maybe you just need some positive feedback about your appearance.

Or: whenever you imagine labor and delivery, you start to panic and wish that you'd never gotten pregnant in the first place. Maybe you need a firm commitment from your mate to be present at the birth. Maybe you need to prepare yourself by researching childbirth education classes. And you probably need some reassurance from your medical provider that you'll go through childbirth and live to tell the tale.

Creating Solutions

Once you know what you need, you can go about thinking of ways to get it. This part of the process involves imagination and a positive attitude.

Maggie needs her husband to be more involved in her pregnancy. She might put him in charge of registering for childbirth education classes. Whenever they're together and the baby starts moving, she might reach for his hand and place it gently on her belly.

Betsy needs her mother to stop nagging her about her weight gain. She might give her mother a brochure on the proper nutritional requirements of pregnancy. Or she might say, "Remember, I'm feeding your grandchild."

Carol needs her doctor to answer her questions. She might schedule a longer appointment. Or she might write down her questions ahead of time and bring copies along for herself and her doctor.

Mimi needs her boss to stop making insensitive jokes. She might bring a note from her doctor stating that pregnancy is not a disability. Or, if necessary, she might remind her employer of the legal ramifications of discrimination and harassment.

One way to keep track of these three steps is by putting them in writing. You may want to include this Clarification Chart in your journal.

FEELINGS	NEEDS	SOLUTIONS

Under *Feelings,* write down a feeling you are having that is bothering you. (Begin the sentence with "I feel . . .")

Under *Needs,* write down a need connected to that feeling. (Begin the sentence with "I need . . .")

Under *Solutions,* write down an action that might satisfy that need. (Begin the sentence with "I could . . .")

Here are some examples of how this process might work:

- "I feel pressured . . . I need more time for relaxation . . . I could ask my mate to take over the cooking for a week."
- "I feel scared . . . I need more information about what's happening to my body during pregnancy . . . I could schedule a consultation with my doctor."
- "I feel anxious . . . I need reassurance at work . . . I could negotiate my maternity leave."

Keep filling in this chart for a period of several weeks. Pay attention to areas in which your needs are changing.

Asking for Support

The chart doesn't include space for step 4 of this process because it's always the same: *doing* whatever is necessary to make your solution a reality. Usually this involves asking for what you want.

For most of us, this is the hard part. But if you don't ask, you don't get; it's as simple as that.

Asking requires both *confidence* and *communication*. You must have confidence that your feelings are valid and you're entitled to have your needs met. And you must communicate in a style most likely to be effective.

Women are famous for taking the indirect route. Instead of saying, "I need more attention," we say, "You never pay any attention to me." Rather than saying, "I need your help," we say, "I guess I shouldn't expect any help from you." Face to face with someone who could give us what we want, we revert to apologies, blaming, or complaining. This in turn makes the other person feel defensive and angry.

Why complicate things and defeat your purpose at the start? Just ask! Do it in a respectful, direct, and positive way, and you'll increase your chances of a favorable outcome. The worst that could happen is that the other person will say no. But even that's preferable to burying your feelings and never acknowledging your needs.

STRENGTHENING YOUR SUPPORT SYSTEMS

Getting your needs met depends on the presence of reliable and effective support systems. Before you became pregnant, you probably had several of these in place and operational. Now it's time to take a closer look at them. Pregnancy has propelled you into a whole new world in which the old ones may not be sufficient anymore; shoring them up is your responsibility.

A pregnant woman's three major support systems are her *mate*, her *medical provider*, and her *work*.

Your Mate

Your mate will be the single most valuable source of support during your pregnancy. After all, this is his baby, too. He is the one person in the world whose investment in your pregnancy is equal to yours.

If your mate is willing and able to affirm your pregnancy and share in its ups and downs, you'll have a far easier time expressing your needs and getting them met. If he isn't, you're likely to feel angry, upset, and alone.

Your mate should be providing four kinds of support: *physical support, reassurance, commitment,* and *respect.* These are present in every loving relationship, but the changes of pregnancy have made your need for them more pressing.

PHYSICAL SUPPORT

If your pregnancy is taking a lot out of you, you'll need some extra help from your mate.

There may be times when you're too sick or exhausted to take care of even the simplest chores. During the times when you're feeling great, there will still be some tasks you won't be able to perform, whether it's pushing furniture around, painting the house, or emptying the kitty litter.

Help in this area is one of the hardest things to ask for. Pregnant women are not invalids! And most of us don't take advantage of the opportunity to be pampered. We've spent years learning how to be independent and not to measure our worth on the basis of our relationships with men. We're afraid of losing ground.

Jeannine has been a runner for years. She's proud of her strength and endurance. But now that she's pregnant, she can hardly move herself off the couch without a push from behind. Her husband is happy to assist her in any way possible, but she resents asking. Her diminished physical capabilities have left her feeling angry at herself.

Whether your mate is open to providing more physical support will depend in part on the existing patterns in your relationship. How have the household chores been divided? Who has traditionally done what? How has your pregnancy affected the way each of you is handling your responsibilities? Is he willing to change his habits and accommodate your needs as a pregnant woman?

Are *you* willing to accept your needs and ask for support? It's a real challenge to maintain your independence while simultaneously allowing yourself to be vulnerable.

Pregnancy requires tremendous physical strength and fortitude. Much of your energy at present is going toward growing a new life. Let your mate help in any way he can.

REASSURANCE

Reassurance is a way of saying, "I understand how you're feeling, and everything will be okay." It's something pregnant women need a lot of.

You need to be told that your body is still okay, that the baby will be okay, and that your feelings are okay. But reassurance is even harder to ask for than help. It seems silly to need this kind of comfort. Shouldn't you be able to handle the changes of pregnancy without seeking constant reassurance? The answer is no.

We all need frequent reassurance. Especially during pregnancy, it's important to have your feelings affirmed and your fears alleviated. A hug, a kind word, and an attentive ear can go a long way toward holding your relationship together and keeping it strong.

COMMITMENT

Commitment is a deep and long-term expression of support. If there was ever a time when you needed commitment from your mate, it's now.

You should feel *absolutely sure* that he's in this with you for the duration. We all fear being alone, and carrying a child intensifies the terror of abandonment.

For most of us, the thought of giving birth and raising a child on our own is not a pleasant one. It's one thing to take care of yourself and quite another to assume sole responsibility for a baby's survival. You were single before, and you probably did just fine, but that was different.

If you're living with the father of your child, be grateful. You can be reasonably confident that he'll be there to see you through the emotional and financial demands of pregnancy and motherhood. Many of our sisters who are single mothers-to-be must look elsewhere for the support you can find in your own home.

What do you need in order to believe that your relationship will provide long-term security? People express commitment in a variety of ways. Not everyone can come right out and say, "I'm with you for eternity." But your mate probably says this in his own language, and it ought to be a language you understand.

One man assumed all the household chores when his wife was pregnant; another took time off work to attend every one of his wife's OB appointments; and still another arrived home one day with dozens of tiny undershirts. Perhaps your mate is putting up the crib and arranging the nursery, or perhaps he's bringing you your favorite Chinese food.

It's important to notice the ways in which he is showing his interest in and commitment to your pregnancy. It's also important to be honest if you're feeling insecure about the firmness of his commitment. Are you having doubts about making it together for the next fifty years? Are his words or actions telling you that he's not as eager for this baby as you'd like him to be? Does he ever say, even jokingly, "You're the one who wanted a baby," or "I guess you won't need me anymore"?

Pregnancy arouses both our positive and negative feelings about commitment. Deciding to have a child together is a statement about the future. It implies permanence and lasting togetherness. You and your mate may be eager to make more solid commitments to each other—or you may each be having some fears about what it means to seal your relationship with a child.

You and your mate have made two major commitments to each other. The first was when you joined your lives; the second was when you decided to have a baby. Each was an act of faith, and each needs to be reaffirmed at various intervals. Pregnancy is a time when your commitment should be spoken, out loud and often.

RESPECT

A respectful attitude toward your pregnancy is an immeasurable source of support. Knowing that your mate appreciates what it means to carry a child can make a big difference in how you experience your pregnancy.

It's very difficult to communicate what pregnancy is like to someone who isn't going through it. Your emotional and physical experiences are almost impossible to put into words. You appreciate the value and significance of what you're doing. Does he?

If he does, then he should be willing to find out what you need and do his best to support you. If he doesn't, then meeting your needs may be hard for him.

Unfortunately, there are men out there who just don't get it. They think that pregnancy is simply something women do, something too ordinary to be deserving of special respect. If this describes the man you're involved with, I urge you to consider your own attitudes toward pregnancy.

Do *you* have the proper reverence for it, or are you taking yourself for granted? To earn the respect of others, we must first respect ourselves. If you share your feelings of self-respect with your mate, he may begin to see the light. But if he continues to view your pregnancy as nothing special, you should then reexamine the values present in your relationship. How does he *really* feel about women? If he doesn't respect your pregnancy, how will he treat you once you become a mother? And what kinds of messages will he send your child?

Your mate's behavior may indicate negative attitudes toward you or the baby (or both). There may be several reasons behind his feelings. The fear of taking responsibility or making a commitment may be causing him to act withdrawn. He may be withholding affection because he's ambivalent about the baby or uncomfortable with your changing image as a mother-to-be.

If you sense that there's something seriously wrong with your relationship, *seek professional help*. It's tempting to ignore problems and hope that they'll disappear once the baby arrives, but it's risky, too. Of course, some men *do* change once the baby is born. While they may not get very involved in the pregnancy, they become much more enthusiastic when they have a "real" baby to hold and relate to. However, there are men who remain uninvolved even after the baby arrives, and in such cases, professional counseling may be the best alternative.

Pregnancy is preparation for becoming a family. Family members depend on one another. Who will get up with the baby when it cries in the middle of the night? How will you reassure each other when you have doubts about your parenting? Are you committed to spending a lifetime together? Will you respect each other as you both continue to grow and change?

Throughout your lives, you'll encounter many more situations in which you need to depend on each other for various kinds of support. Strengthening your bonds now will serve you well later, as you join hands in raising your child.

Your Medical Provider

Some women end up unhappy with their relationships with their medical providers, and often they don't know why. In most cases, the issue is power—or, more specifically, the lack of it, as far as women are concerned.

Power, be it solar, electrical, or personal, is what makes things happen. It's the spark that ignites, illuminates, and drives us. During my first pregnancy, I had almost no power, primarily because I had almost no self-confidence. I couldn't get my needs met because I didn't know how to ask for help. Everything was new. The medical information was foreign to me, and the physiological changes were frightening. But instead of speaking up, I accepted this situation as normal. I assumed that it's all right to wait nearly an hour and then see your doctor for a total of twelve minutes. I assumed that books would answer my questions and friends would calm my fears. I simply didn't know any better.

Here's what I've learned since then: Your medical provider can give you a great deal of support, *if you expect it and ask for it.* If you had the flu, you'd certainly let your doctor or midwife know. Why not also get help with your emotional health?

To repeat—this is a power issue. Power plays a part in any relationship. Who's in charge? Who calls the shots? Who makes the decisions? In your relationship with your medical provider, this power should pass back and forth between the two of you. He or she has the training, but *you* have the inside story.

We've all been taught to perceive doctors as omnipotent. If we have a problem, they have the answer; if we're sick, they have the cure. And they do deserve respect; they study long and hard to practice their profession, and in some cases, their skills make the difference between life and death. *But they aren't gods.*

Too often, we give them *all* the power and reserve none for ourselves. We become passive and intimidated in the face of their knowledge. We hesitate to call them with "minor" complaints. (How often have you held back from asking a question you think might be silly?) Of course a doctor's time is precious. But what about *your* time? What about *your* needs?

Attitudes are changing. As we become more educated consumers, we're learning that our needs matter and our demands bring results. Obstetrics and gynecology is now an extremely competitive business in the United States. The increase in HMOs (health maintenance organizations) is forcing private-practice physicians to become more sensitive to serving their patients' needs. Midwives are setting up shop in clinics and hospitals. Women today have a choice—and with choice comes power.

Your medical provider should offer the kind of support *you* need. This is *your* body, *your* baby, and *your* pregnancy. You know better than anyone how you feel and how your baby is doing. Your internal sense of yourself is the best diagnostic tool around. Trust it. Take back your power. A supportive medical provider will welcome and encourage you to do so.

Your Work

Having a job while being pregnant is a mixed blessing. It keeps your cash flowing, your mind busy, and your thoughts on something besides yourself and the baby. It provides you with financial independence, self-esteem, and a social network.

But it's also just plain *difficult* to do. The demands of your job may seem far greater than usual. Thoughts of the baby may distract you. Your body is working on a big project and meeting deadlines of its own that have nothing to do with a nine-to-five routine.

In addition, you may feel alienated being pregnant in a professional milieu. Our culture isn't yet accustomed to pregnant women making sales presentations, conducting meetings, and striding down the corridors of corporate headquarters. We still do a double-take whenever we see a flight attendant whose belly precedes the rest of her down the aisle.

Years ago, working while one was pregnant wasn't an issue because it usually wasn't done. Those women who did have jobs retired as soon as they started showing. But today more than 50 percent of all women who were working when they became pregnant choose to continue their careers.[1]

The fact that they can do so is one sign that our long, hard fight for equality in the workplace is paying off. It doesn't mean that our struggle is over, however. Women are still underpaid (earning 64 cents to every dollar men earn[2]) and underpowerful (men hold most influential positions), and the right to maternity leave is not yet law.

The economic demands of carrying and raising a child make working a necessity for most of us. But while many women are glad to keep working well into their pregnancies, an equal number wish that there was no such thing as a pinstriped maternity suit.

Some women feel compelled to carry on with as much resolve and energy as before. Debbie, a research assistant, describes the pressures of working while pregnant: "I have no intention of proving the saying, A woman's place is in the home. But even though I'm determined to keep pulling my weight, being pregnant *has* hampered my ability to work, in some ways. I tire more easily, and my concentration is at an all-time low. Morning sickness has made me late more often than usual. Frankly, there are times when I resent having to act as if nothing has changed."

Other women see pregnancy as an opportunity to relax their expectations of themselves. While you may continue to be as motivated as ever, being pregnant may diminish your job's importance in your life. As you blend your career with motherhood, keeping your job in perspective may prove to be an ongoing challenge. Right now you may be willing to work on weekends or bring work home with you; as a mother, you may place a higher value on having flexible hours and time with your child. Currently you may rely a great deal on your employer's impression of you; once you have a child, your self-esteem may be less dependent on your job performance.

Your work is your third major support system. You spend a large proportion of your waking hours at your job, giving it what you can. Are you getting from it what you need?

You should be finding three kinds of support in your workplace: *acceptance, accommodation,* and *respect.*

ACCEPTANCE

Acceptance involves more than just the acknowledgment of your pregnancy. That should come almost automatically; no one can ignore that your pregnant body exists.

The *real* issue is one of how you're being treated. How are people responding to your pregnancy? Is your employer supportive of your needs? Are your co-workers genuinely sympathetic toward the changes you're experiencing? Are people still soliciting your opinion and input on important matters?

Accepting you as a pregnant woman is one thing; accepting you as a mother-to-be is another. Pregnant women are often asked, "How are you going to keep working after your baby is born?" It's assumed that the father of your child will combine parenthood with his career; why shouldn't you be able to do the same?

Most of us have been raised to believe that "real men" bring home the bacon while "real women" stay at home with the children. Whether or not we admit it, we still believe this to some extent. Working women are perceived as brazen, aggressive, even "masculine"—qualities that conflict with our images of soft, nurturing mothers.

We're confused, and this confusion makes it difficult to be assertive in the workplace. We're afraid of losing ground and relinquishing the rights we've worked so hard to get.

The key to winning acceptance in the workplace is to accept *yourself*. If you ever feel yourself weakening, repeat one (or all) of the following to yourself:

- "I have the right to keep working during my pregnancy."
- "I have the right to have a baby without jeopardizing my career."
- "I'm not just any employee—I'm a pregnant employee."

ACCOMMODATION

In our society, people's worth is based largely on their productivity. Unfortunately, producing new lives doesn't seem to count.

As T. Berry Brazelton writes in his book *On Becoming a Family,* "There is an implicit put-down in the professional world for women who must stop what they are doing to have and nurture a baby. We do not offer sanctions for women to stop their careers temporarily without losing out on their opportunities."[3]

The United States lags far behind other nations in accommodating pregnancy and motherhood in the workplace. We feel this lack of accommodation as we spend our much-needed lunch hours at our OB appointments and save up our vacation time to use as maternity leave.

Right now you need greater flexibility at work. You should be able to take more frequent breaks. You shouldn't be doing heavy physical labor. You should be able to get what you need without being patronized, penalized, or discriminated against. If all this qualifies as "special treatment"—something pregnant women are wary of asking for—then so be it. Unless everyone you work with is also pregnant, you *are* special.

Some employers will go out of their way to adjust to the needs of their pregnant employees. Most, however, will not—and some will try to make things more difficult. Discrimination, both subtle and blatant, is all around us. No wonder we worry about asking for "favors." No wonder we feel that we have to work harder than men to protect our position.

Brenda was one month pregnant when she decided to look for a new job. She interviewed for a position as a receptionist, and she thought she had made a very good impression. Her work history was impeccable, her references were excellent, and she was more than qualified. At the end of the interview, she was offered the job and accepted it.

Then she mentioned that she was expecting a baby in the spring. Following a lengthy silence, her prospective boss cleared his throat and said, "Well, we do have a few other candidates to interview. We'll be in touch." She never heard from him again.

Once more, it all comes back to power. As pregnant working women, we feel powerless and we hesitate to make waves. We give up our rights and we suffer the consequences. Discrimination is hard to fight, and we haven't been trained as fighters. We keep quiet when we ought to speak up; we sit down when we should take action.

The refusal to accommodate to your changing needs is a form of discrimination. You have the right to continue working without sacrificing your physical and emotional well-being. Stand up for yourself!

RESPECT

Do your employer and co-workers act as if they respect your pregnancy? Do they perceive what you're doing as valuable? If so, hold on to your job for dear life. You're in a progressive work environment, and those are few and far between.

Having a baby shakes up the system. Babies are gifts to the

world, but the contributions of childbearing women still go largely unrecognized.

It's especially important right now for you to respect *yourself* and what you're doing. Let your self-respect show, and the people around you may catch on.

NEGOTIATING YOUR MATERNITY LEAVE

You need acceptance, accommodation, and respect from your employer and your co-workers during your pregnancy. Even without them, however, you'll still be able to function.

The one thing you absolutely *won't* be able to do without is maternity leave. That baby is on its way, and unless you plan on giving birth at your desk, you're going to have to make arrangements.

Negotiating is not something most women are particularly well-equipped to do. Instead, we've been taught to comply, cooperate, and capitulate. Perhaps this is one area in which we could take a lesson from men. According to traditional male strategy, the negotiating process involves three steps. Let's apply each of these to the maternity leave issue.

1. *Know your bottom line.* In female language, this means knowing what you need. Will you want six months off, or will you want to return to work two weeks after the baby is born? How can you possibly tell at this stage of the game?

   You're going to have to decide. Consider what you want, and then balance this against the realities of your job. Try to find a point somewhere in the middle. Then be prepared to ask for more!

2. *Present your opening position.* Here's where you'll assert your needs. Before doing this, though, you'll need to know the facts.

   What's company policy on maternity leaves? If it has been written down somewhere, get a copy and familiarize yourself with it. If it hasn't, find out what precedents have been set. Talk to other mothers in your company to determine what you can reasonably expect.

3) *Bargain*. Men refer to this stage as getting down to brass tacks. Think of it as a communication process in which you present your arguments, you listen to your employer's responses, and then you both describe what you want.

For example, you might say, "I will need two months off in order to be completely recovered and ready to give my job the energy it requires." Your employer might respond, "Six weeks would be okay, but I'll need you back by the end of August." At this point, you start compromising.

Be creative! Is there someone in the office you could train to cover for you? Could you revise your schedule to complete an important project before the baby arrives? Is it possible for you to work from home for a couple of weeks?

Strive for a "win-win" situation—one in which you *both* get what you need. Try to compromise in such a way that *neither* of you feels taken advantage of or disappointed.

Throughout this process, remind yourself of your power as an employee. You are of value to your company. It's in your employer's best interests to keep you working, and it's to your advantage to come up with a solution that's mutually satisfying.

Learning how to get what you need is a lifelong process. As newborn babies, we all start out keenly aware of our needs to be fed, nurtured, and cared for. As we get older, we learn to stifle our needs, to stop asking for what we want, and to settle for a lot less.

Pregnancy offers the opportunity to change this—for now, and for later. The built-in vulnerability of carrying a child makes it necessary to ask for support. This isn't a bad habit to get into; unmet needs are the stuff of which miserable lives are made.

If you face your needs now and learn what it takes to satisfy them, you'll be on your way to a more satisfying life. And this will make a difference in every one of your relationships: as lover, sister, daughter, and friend, you'll be more able to give *and* take.

You'll be a better mother, too. If you take this time to discover your needs, you'll enter motherhood as a whole person, not a martyr. Many of us have mothers whose lives have been filled with recriminations and regret. They've expected their children to make up for what they never had. This doesn't have to happen to you. Learn to nurture and care for yourself, and you'll be that much more capable of loving your child.

FOR MEDICAL PROVIDERS

I speak to you both as a patient and as someone who has spoken with hundreds of pregnant women. I have heard about what they are and aren't getting in the area of maternity care. Many of them like and trust their doctors—and just as many feel angry and frustrated at the lack of support they receive.

If they could speak with all of you, here is what they'd say:

- *"We want more than medical supervision."*

  They also need *information*—facts about what's happening to them and why. But they often perceive you as being busy and harried, and they're afraid to ask too many questions. Some of them don't know the right questions to ask.

  How can you help? By listening, thoughtfully and sincerely. By hearing their unspoken concerns. And by asking *them* questions about how they're doing.

- *"We need more time and attention—not just medically, but also in regard to our feelings."*

  Pregnant women experience a wide range of emotions that can be frightening and confusing. They need you to examine these as carefully as you examine their bodies. They need reassurance, and they need to have their fears put into perspective. Since you see and talk with pregnant women every day, you're in a unique position to help. You have the experience to give them reassurance and settle their insecurities and fears.

• *"We need your respect."*

How do you speak to your patients? What tone of voice do you use? Do you treat them as equals?

How well do you listen? How do you respond when someone asks the same question you've heard a million times before?

How do you really *feel* about women? Pregnant women are extremely sensitive; they pick up on the slightest hint of being patronized or discounted.

How respectful is your behavior? Do you call a pregnant woman by her first name, yet expect her to address you as "doctor"? Do you wait until she's fully dressed and facing you before carrying on meaningful discussions, or do you talk to her while she's flat on her back, undressed, exposed, and feeling vulnerable? Which of these have you communicated: that you'll be delivering the baby, or that you'll be happy to assist as she births her child?

You're in the business of serving pregnant women. To succeed over the long haul, you'll need to provide full service to your patients' emotional needs as well as their physical ones. Talk to your patients and find out what they need—not just for their sake, but for yours as well. They can help you become better at what you do.

FOR EMPLOYERS

What was your first reaction when your employee told you that she was pregnant? Did you think, "Great—she's going to be a mother," or "Oh, no, what's this going to cost me?"

Most women experience some apprehension about continuing to work during pregnancy. Their physical needs are imposing, and they're reluctant to ask for flexibility (much less for caring and concern). They're also fearful about negotiating maternity leave.

Has pregnancy changed her value in your eyes? Will her efforts to combine work with motherhood jeopardize her career?

Consider your attitudes toward pregnant women. Do you think they belong in the workplace? What about mothers? Do you believe that you can count on a working mother to be responsible and dependable? How are you communicating these attitudes?

If you are genuinely supportive of your pregnant employee, does she know it, or are you keeping it a secret? Do you ever ask her how her pregnancy is going? What would it say to her if *you* were the one to organize a baby shower rather than leaving it up to her co-workers?

Review your company's maternity leave policies. Do they seem reasonable? Do they work out to most people's satisfaction? Are you in a position to set or change such policy to make it more flexible?

Have you taken the initiative to work out her maternity leave? Would you consider allowing her to job-share once the baby is born? Are you willing to keep her informed of what's going on in her absence? A written maternity leave contract is one way to protect both of you.

If your employee is valuable to you—if you want to keep her now and after the baby arrives—you'll need to accommodate the changes in her life. If you support her now, you'll be helping to build a long-term, loyal relationship that can pay off for years to come.

7

"I'm Not Fat, I'm Pregnant!"

Being pregnant is a lot like being a movie star. The whole world watches. Everyone wants to know the date of the big premiere, and strangers come out of nowhere to touch you.

Unfortunately, that's where the similarities end. Pregnancy doesn't bring fame and fortune. There's no chauffeured limousine to drive you to the doctor, and you have to wait your turn at the supermarket just like everyone else. Dark glasses don't begin to disguise you, and no solicitous aides hover to answer your phone, turn away unwanted callers, and otherwise protect your privacy.

Like it or not, *everyone* notices a pregnant woman.

When I was expecting, a friend of mine remarked, "It must be great to be pregnant. You don't have to worry about how you look anymore. For nine months, you can stop competing with all those fashionably svelte women."

Is that true? Does pregnancy provide a respite from the pressure to look perfect? Yes—and no.

You don't have to hold in your tummy anymore. (I'd been

holding mine in for so long that it was practically a reflex.) On the other hand, you're always on display. Wherever you go, whatever you do, people stare. Sometimes they comment loudly enough for you to hear. They even say things to your face!

I never stopped worrying about my appearance. I just worried about different aspects of it. I did stop trying to look like a fashion model; that seemed pointless. Instead, I substituted my image of the Perfect Pregnant Woman: glowing complexion, no stretch marks, and a beautifully shaped belly out front.

Where does this image come from? Why are *all* pregnant women supposed to have that legendary glow? If you're radiant, it may mean that you're happy and healthy and your pregnancy becomes you. If you're not, it certainly doesn't mean that there's anything wrong with you or your appearance.

And where did we get the idea that looking good while pregnant means showing only in front? The twenty to fifty pounds you gain isn't all going to pack itself neatly around the baby. Yet we all hope that no one will be able to tell we're pregnant from the back (unless we walk funny).

With that image and its demands, we're all doomed to disappointment from the outset. Actually we're doomed long before then. Very few women, pregnant or not, are completely satisfied with their appearance at *any* stage of life. Each of us is too short, too tall, too round, or too flat; too big, too small, too thin, or too fat. We're trapped in a never-ending search for the "right look." And we don't have to search very far: We're constantly reminded of the cultural emphasis on youth and beauty, and we're inundated by media images of women who are five feet eleven inches tall and weigh 115 pounds. (Have you ever seen a model who looked as if she'd had a baby? Are their bodies made of elastic?)

Pregnancy intensifies our interest in our appearance. We think about it almost as much as we think about the baby. Be honest —how often have you asked yourself (or your mate) any of these questions?

"Do I look any different?"

"Am I still pretty?"

"Am I too big?"

"Am I too small?"

"Do I look fat?"

"Can you tell from the back?"

Asking those questions doesn't mean that you're vain, insecure, or obsessed with yourself. It's perfectly natural to be more focused on your body now than you ever were before. The changes occurring in it are exciting and interesting to behold. Besides, how can you possibly ignore what's happening (literally) in front of you? Your body is the most vivid manifestation of your pregnancy. The fact that it's blossoming is one sure sign that the baby is developing as it should.

Still, it is strange to watch your body get bigger (and bigger, and bigger). How you experience these changes will depend in part on how you feel physically. If you feel ungainly or as if your body is no longer your own, it is difficult to perceive yourself as healthy and in tip-top shape. The physical discomforts of pregnancy may make it seem as if your body isn't working the way it should be.

On the other hand, you may enjoy the sensation of being swept away by what's happening inside you. This may be the first time in your life that you haven't had to fret about how much you eat or what you weigh. It may be a big relief to finally let it all hang out.

At the same time, you're probably concerned about bringing it all back in when your pregnancy is over. You've heard how hard it is to lose those last ten pounds, and we've all seen women who have looked dumpy and dowdy for the rest of their lives after having a baby. None of us wants to end up like that.

But that's the future; this is *now*. And your pregnancy is definitely growing on you.

FEMININE OR FAT?

The two words pregnant women most often use to describe their bodies are "feminine" and "fat." Each means something entirely different.

"Feminine" conjures images of roundness, softness, and ripeness. It implies an overall pride in having a female body. It's a *positive* word.

"Fat," with all due respect to the big, beautiful women of the world, is just the opposite. It implies sloppiness and overindulgence.

Calling someone feminine is a compliment; calling someone fat is an insult.

Whether you perceive the changes in your body as feminine or fat has a lot to do with your past relationship to your body. Starting during childhood, and later, over the years, you've developed a picture of the way you look. Were you a cute baby, or did you have a face that only a mother could love? Did people say that you were a pretty little girl, or did they promise that you'd be pretty when you grew up? Did you attract attention from boys, or did you hide in the bathroom at parties? These memories have combined to create a lasting self-image.

Pregnancy arouses those memories all over again. If weight has been a problem for you in the past, you may be feeling some anxiety as you watch the number of pregnancy pounds climb on the scale. If you were a teenager who wore layers of Clearasil to bed each night, you're probably examining your skin for those funny brown patches you've read about. If you wore a training bra until you were fifteen, you may be fixated on watching your breasts ripen and swell.

Whatever you felt about yourself before is affecting your reactions to having a pregnant body. This is true on the positive side as well. If you've always enjoyed your body's sensuality, you'll appreciate the extra sensitivity of your skin. If you've prized your curves ever since they started forming, you'll welcome the added blossoming of pregnancy. But if the rounded Earth Mother look conflicts with your notion of sex appeal, you may be less pleased.

What do you see when you look at yourself? The next time you're alone in the house, take off all your clothes and stand in front of the mirror. Examine yourself from head to toe. Turn sideways. Again. Then look at your back from over your shoulder.

When you're through, take out your journal and answer these questions:

1. How often do you look in the mirror? Now that you're pregnant, are you surprised by what you see?
2. Are you aware of other people looking at you? How do you think they would describe your body?
3. Does your mate think you're beautiful? Does he think you're sexy?
4. Do you like the shape of your belly? Or do you think it's too big, or too small?
5. How do you feel about the amount of weight you've gained? Do you think you look feminine, or fat?
6. What do you like least about your pregnant body? What do you like most about it?

Continue to ask yourself these questions at various intervals along the way. Pay attention to how your answers evolve.

Few women are totally at ease with the physical transformations that accompany pregnancy. Your reflection in the mirror may raise some very ambivalent feelings. If you find it difficult to integrate the reality of your pregnant body into your idea of attractiveness, it's no wonder. You'd be hard pressed to find popular images that present pregnant women in this light. Have you ever seen an ad for a romantic cruise featuring a pregnant woman and her mate? How about a television commercial with a pregnant woman draped across the hood of a car? Is the confident New Woman—the "banker you can trust"—ever pregnant?

Pregnant women are becoming more visible in the public eye and the workplace, but pregnancy continues to be portrayed as incompatible with glamour, success, or romance. The expectant mother is typically shown clutching a box of diapers or gazing dreamily into space with her hands gently folded across her stomach. She is rarely if ever seen as a sleek, sharp woman on the move. If perceiving yourself as still sexy and attractive is a problem, the stereotypes may be getting in your way.

Your body image is also affected by your mate's response. Some men are genuinely attracted to pregnant women; others are not. And the reactions of either may fluctuate at different stages along the way.

If you're disappointed by your mate's seeming lack of sensitivity, remember that he, too, has been influenced by the stereotypes. It may take time for him to adjust to the radical changes in your appearance. Or he may simply be the kind of man who is turned off by the sight of pregnancy. This doesn't—repeat, doesn't—mean that he loves you any less. Even so, embarrassed silences or jokes are poor substitutes for the adoration you'd hoped for, and they certainly don't help you feel good about yourself.

Fortunately, pregnancy doesn't last forever. You may have to accept his feelings and trust that his attraction will be rekindled once the baby is born.

There are other men, though, who truly believe that pregnant women are beautiful. If your mate says this of you, accept it (and rejoice!). Don't let your own negative feelings prevent you from enjoying his sincere compliments. It's utterly self-defeating to suggest that he have his vision checked when he insists that he likes the way you look. Chances are he means it. (Even if he doesn't, and he's just saying it to cheer you up, why argue?)

Ultimately, *your* attitude is the one that counts. If *you're* convinced that pregnant women are sexless, fat, or dowdy, then you're probably communicating this message to the people around you. And this self-effacing attitude may be reflected in a lack of concern for your appearance.

Pregnancy doesn't have to be an obstacle to self-esteem, and it shouldn't be an excuse to stop caring about the way you look. In fact, it can be an opportunity to enhance your appearance. Since your body is changing anyway, why not give your image a boost? Maybe now is the time to experiment with makeup or update your hairstyle. When you shop for maternity clothes, try different colors from those you usually wear. Have a manicure or a massage. Even if you're not interested in creating a whole new look, it's essential to take pride in your appearance.

What kind of statement are *you* making as a pregnant woman? Are you reinforcing the stereotypes—or challenging them by looking your best?

WHOSE BODY IS IT, ANYWAY?

The way other people see you will contribute to your self-image. The added attention may flatter and delight you, or it may be embarrassing suddenly to be in the spotlight.

During the early stages of my pregnancies, I liked being noticed. I wanted to be sure that *everyone* was aware of my condition. Later on, though, I became irritated by the constant attention and interest in my body. I felt like a laboratory specimen.

Comments like "Eating for two?" "You're carrying low; it must be a boy!" and "How's the little mother today?" get old fast. Even if they're meant to express caring, they may make you feel patronized and pressured. *Obviously* you're eating for two. Maybe you want a *girl*, not a boy. And, naturally you're not *little* —you're bigger than you've ever been in your life!

It's best to ignore remarks like these. Or smile and change the subject. You know how much to eat and how much weight you're willing to gain. The baby is in the proper position wherever it is, and the way you're carrying it has nothing to do with its gender. And there's nothing "little" about you, your baby, or the emotional journey of pregnancy.

But what should you do about the genuine boors—the people who persist in saying stupid things? Your pregnancy doesn't give them the right to be disrespectful or overstep your personal boundaries. Nobody should think of walking up to complete strangers and touching them without permission. Under any other circumstances, it would be rude and inappropriate for anyone besides your mate or a close friend to ask you how much you weigh. Yet these things happen to pregnant women all the time.

Babies don't belong to the world, pregnant women aren't public property, and even though your body is growing a baby, *it still belongs to you*. And it's up to you to set limits on what other people say about it (and do to it).

We've all seen T-shirts proclaiming "Baby Under Construction," with arrows pointing downward (as if people couldn't tell). Which of the following messages would *you* wear?

DON'T TOUCH ME WITHOUT ASKING	LOOK UP— I'M STILL HERE!
I'M NOT FAT— I'M PREGNANT!	BE GENTLE I'M CARRYING A LIFE
I'M STILL SEXY	PREGNANT AND PROUD OF IT
I EXPECT RESPECT	

Why not get it printed on a T-shirt and wear it around? Or, better yet, make up one of your own.

SHOPPING: *A Serious Subject*

You may think that clothes are a trivial matter, considering the importance of everything else you're going through at the moment. Wrong! How you look has a definite impact on how you feel about yourself, and much of that depends on how you're dressed.

Maternity clothes are at the top of every pregnant woman's list of favorite topics. Women talk about where to buy maternity clothes *before* discussing due dates, labor and delivery, and motherhood. Unless you're very different from the rest of us, what you wear can help you feel especially attractive, or it can have the potential to ruin your day. Clothes don't make the woman, but they certainly make a difference.

When I first learned that I was pregnant, two things immediately came to mind: tent dresses and pants with stretchy fronts. I'm not talking about beautiful, flowing smocks or designer jeans with hidden panels; I mean the *ugly* fashions of days long past (thank goodness). Thinking that these were still the norm, I made plans to keep squeezing into my regular clothes for as long as I could. I dug up pants and tops I'd hidden away from my "fat" days, and stocked up on giant safety pins.

I promised myself that I wouldn't shop for maternity clothes until I was twelve weeks pregnant. I made it all the way to two weeks after hearing "It's positive!" before beelining to the nearest maternity shop.

I was determined to find the Perfect Maternity Dress. I didn't look the least bit pregnant, and I wondered if I should be carrying a note from my doctor. I pushed open the door and walked in.

I was amazed at what I saw. There were no tent dresses in sight, and the stretch-front pants had caught up with the eighties. They'd turned into fashionable sweat pants that looked as if anyone could wear them.

Then I noticed the bows. There were bows *everywhere*. Big flowing ones, medium-size ones, and little teeny ones. The majority of them were strategically placed right below the chin.

For some reason, I thought a lot about those bows (and still do). Are they supposed to symbolize demureness, as opposed to sexiness? Or are they meant to draw a viewer's attention away from the stomach and up to the face? To me, they were "cute," and being cute was the last thing that interested me.

I finally found a dress I wanted to try on. It didn't have a bow, but it was *huge*. Nothing I did made it look right on me. I pulled out the front as far as my arms would stretch. (There was still some left over.) Would I ever be that big?

To end the suspense: I bought it. I took it home. I visited it daily, trying to imagine how it would fit once I really started showing. It hung in my closet for three months before I could wear it without appearing ridiculous.

That may have been my first shopping trip for maternity clothes, but it certainly wasn't my last. Over the next several weeks, I was surprised, and discouraged, at the high cost of such items as simple little dresses and unspectacular pants.

I purchased a few carefully chosen items before realizing that there had to be a better way. Very few pregnant women I knew could afford to buy an entire wardrobe of maternity clothes, yet most of them dressed well. I started calling around, to my sister and some close friends.

They offered me their maternity clothes. Terrific, I said, and loaned them some of my regular clothes in exchange. We all ended up with something to wear that was new to us; we all saved money.

I also heard about a maternity consignment shop in town. I ran right over and found several great bargains. I could justify spending fifteen to twenty dollars for a dress or jumper, and I liked the fact that another pregnant woman had worn it before.

Then I discovered Indian and Mexican boutiques, where I bought some of my favorite dresses. The fabrics were light and comfortable, the styles were loose enough to fit, and they didn't look like maternity clothes.

I learned a few things about dressing during pregnancy that I wish someone had told me, and that you may find helpful:

- I tried for much too long to pour myself into my regular clothes. Don't! Why disguise your pregnancy? The minute you start showing (or even before), regular clothes won't fit and they won't look good.
- Clothes I bought at eight weeks never made it to the third trimester. Think big! If something turns out to be *much* too large, you can always take it in.
- Your breasts may get a lot bigger. You'll be wearing a more supportive bra than usual, so avoid spaghetti straps and see-through fabrics.
- After months of living in those Indian and Mexican dresses and a pair of purple sweat pants, I never wanted to see them again. I gave them to a friend who was just *thinking* about having a baby. Pregnancy is no time to add to your permanent wardrobe.
- I bought far too many things and ended up wearing only half of them; the rest I could have lived without. Avoid impulse shopping. Maternity clothes are expensive and very short-lived. Once you get your shape back, the last thing you'll want to do is drape it in something oversize.
- Don't automatically discard everything in your closet. Elastic panels can be inserted into pants, jeans, and even bras to make them wearable during pregnancy.

The key to successful maternity shopping is dressing for yourself. Buy items that feel good and fit well; if you're not comfortable in something, you won't wear it. Forget about what's fashionable and wear what's really *you*. There are enough choices these days for you to express your individuality. A few more tips:

- If you're the casual type, forget the bows. Buy a well-fitting pair of maternity jeans and some big, comfy tops.
- If you're the dress-up type, buy at least one outfit you can wear out on the town and feel smashing in.
- If you spend most of your time at work, buy clothes that will help you feel self-assured in a professional setting. Here's where the money can really add up, but it's worth it. There are plenty of attractive suits, jumpers, and dresses for pregnant working women.
- Shop around until you find something you like; don't settle for less. Designers are finally realizing that women don't lose all sense of taste as soon as they lose their waistlines. Many maternity clothes these days are genuinely stylish. (But don't compare your maternity clothes to Princess Di's. Nobody has a wardrobe like that!)

Ultimately, it's what's *inside* that counts. If you don't feel pretty, the most beautiful dress won't change that. If you like the way you look, almost anything will do. If you're happy, healthy, and secure about your appearance, your beauty will radiate from within, and flattering clothes will only make it more apparent.

YOU LOOK TERRIFIC!

Most of us are engaged in an ongoing process of learning to accept ourselves. We have been culturally conditioned to be critical of our bodies, and we're constantly working at building our self-esteem.

Pregnancy can be a turning point. It was for me. The way I relate to my body has changed enormously because of my pregnancies. Nothing else in my life has contributed so much to my positive feelings about the way I look.

This doesn't mean that I was a raving beauty all through my

pregnancy. At times I looked great, and at other times I didn't. What changed was my image of myself as a woman.

I found out that my body really *works*. Step by step, with or without my help, it was building a baby. The most advanced technology couldn't begin to come close to what my body was accomplishing.

Being pregnant gave me respect for my body's complexity and efficiency; giving birth put me in awe of its strength. I will never again view myself as a clothes hanger. I know now that I'm much more than that.

Having a pregnant body was important in other ways, too. People smile at pregnant women whether they're short, tall, thin, or fat. For the first time in my life, I felt like a perfect 10. I stuck out where I was supposed to and enjoyed eating without worrying about my weight. I saw myself thirty-five pounds heavier, and I still looked like *me*. (The thought of ten extra pounds doesn't scare me anymore.)

I also felt special for nine solid months—as if I belonged to an elite group: the group of pregnant women around the world. It seemed as if we were all spiritually connected. We had something in common, and we were doing something no man could ever do.

If *you* don't think *you're* beautiful, take another look. Regardless of its shape, size, or features, your body is evidence of the miracle of creation. No wonder primitive cultures used to worship images of pregnant women. No wonder the big-bellied, big-breasted Earth Mother has been such a powerful icon since the beginning of time.

You can go through your pregnancy self-conscious and embarrassed, or you can be proud of your gorgeous, blooming body. Why carry yourself with any less dignity than you carry your baby? Take this opportunity to love and appreciate your body, and these feelings will endure for the rest of your life.

8

Is Three a Crowd?

In your present condition, sex may seem like a sensitive, sore, or sensational subject. But sex and pregnancy are so intimately linked that you can't explore one without at least thinking about the other. After all, unless your baby is a miracle of modern technology, sex is what *got* you pregnant.

How is pregnancy affecting your sexual relationship with your mate? Do you still think you're sexy? Do you care?

This chapter is about personal questions and answers—questions that may be bothering you, and answers that I hope will help.

SEX AND SEXUALITY

Let's start by defining terms. By "sex" I mean the sexual relationship you have with your mate and the way you express your sexual feelings in that relationship. By "sexuality" I mean the way you experience yourself as a sexual being.

Pregnancy affects both your sexuality and your sexual relationship. For one thing, it announces to the world that you've been sexual at least once. You may look sweet and innocent, or you may have a no-nonsense, businesslike air that implies that sex is the furthest thing from your mind, but none of that matters. You know, and everyone else knows that you know.

Sexuality is always a highly individual matter, and pregnant women run the gamut in describing theirs. Some feel sexier, more attractive, and more easily aroused than ever before in their lives. Others are completely turned off by the mere thought of sex; they don't feel the least bit sexy, and they couldn't be less interested in the act.

There are several factors that may be influencing the way you feel about your sexuality. First and foremost is the baby. You're continuously aware of its presence, and that may be causing both sensory and emotional overload. Many women are drawn inward to the incredible drama of creation taking place within their bodies. When compared to that, everything else may pale.

The physical changes of pregnancy, especially those that occur during the first and third trimesters, may alter your level of sexual desire. If you're experiencing fatigue, nausea, or extreme tenderness in your breasts, sex may be the last thing on your mind. The fear of miscarriage may cause you to shy away from lovemaking. During the final months, sheer bulk or anxieties about labor and delivery may stifle your interest in sex.

On the plus side, pregnancy may result in a heightened awareness of your body. You're more in touch with how it moves, smells, looks, and feels. For some women, pregnancy is a powerful aphrodisiac. Their sexuality is enhanced by the fact of their own fertility. If this is true for you, then you may experience increased sensitivity and pleasure during lovemaking, and you may also feel freer and less inhibited. Because the barriers (and worries) of birth control have been removed, you may be more physically and emotionally open to your mate.

Or you may perceive the baby's presence as an obstacle. Some women hesitate to be intimate for fear of hurting themselves or the baby.

Meredith recently gave birth to her first child. "Especially during the last trimester, I felt weird about making love," she recalls. "First, there were those two imaginary eyes staring at me. I had read books, I had talked to my doctor, I had tried reasoning with myself, but I was still convinced that the baby was watching! And if it was sleeping, we were certainly waking it up. My own child *knew* I was having sex, and it just wasn't right.

"I was also terrified of hurting it. Again, I knew better, but I still had this image of a head-on collision between my husband and the baby.

"Then there were the logistical problems. The old positions were too difficult, and the new ones made me feel like an oversize Nadia Comaneci on the verge of a serious fall.

"And finally, when I was lying on my back, I couldn't even see my feet, much less anything else that was happening south of my navel. So I felt removed and squeamish about being touched."

In addition to all this is the realization that *you're about to become a mother*. Every time the baby moves, kicks, or stretches, you're reminded that you're no longer the person you used to be. Each facet of your identity is changing, including your sexuality. The feelings of awe and wonder that come from carrying your baby may enhance your female self-image—or the stereotype of matronly mothers may prevent you from seeing yourself as sexy, attractive, and exciting.

Pregnancy is a transition, a time when you're gradually developing a brand-new part of yourself—the mother part. Right now you're forming an attachment to your child that will endure for the rest of your life and that evokes strong feelings of responsibility and protectiveness. Being a mother implies the need to grow up and settle down, and this stands in sharp contrast to the freedom and spontaneity we usually associate with sexiness.

Although conception itself is a sexual act, mothers are rarely considered sexy. The historic ideal is the serene madonna, the provider of sustenance and nurturing whose complacent composure is the opposite of sexual passion or lust. The story of the Immaculate Conception is itself a powerful statement of nonsexual motherhood. Even if it isn't part of your religious upbringing, it may subconsciously color your sexuality, leaving you feeling uncomfortable or guilty.

Modern notions of motherhood are not much different, especially as depicted in the media. Remember the moms you grew up with on television? There was the one in the commercial, bandana tied around her head, cheerfully discussing the pros and cons of toilet cleaners. There was June Cleaver in her high-necked flowered frock, starched apron, and pumps. There was Lucy, announcing her pregnancy at the Tropicana Club; we celebrated her news, suffered through her morning sickness, and anxiously awaited the birth of Little Ricky—while she and Desi continued to sleep in separate beds.

And what about your own mother? You may think she's beautiful, you may admire her greatly, but would you describe her as sexy? Probably not. You yourself are proof of her sexuality, but can you imagine her and your father making love?

It's important to be aware of your own view of mothers and how it is affecting your sexuality. If you buy into the idea that motherhood and sexiness are mutually exclusive, your sexual identity may suffer. New mothers often say that the shift to full-time caregiver is so radical that they stop thinking of themselves as sexual beings. Their children's needs and demands are so consuming that it's impossible to deal with anything else.

Having children makes it virtually impossible to focus solely on yourself. In the past, you may have taken an hour to bathe and fuss in front of the mirror prior to a night out with your mate. A year from now, you may find yourself getting dressed in between giving instructions to the sitter and extricating yourself from little fingers sticky with peanut butter. But that doesn't mean you can't look fabulous just the same.

And becoming a mother doesn't mean the end of your life as a beautiful, sexy woman. Carrying and bearing a child can actually be an opportunity to enrich your sexual identity. Over time, you may discover that you're everything you once were—and more.

STAYING CLOSE TO YOUR MATE

How are you two doing, anyway? Are you continuing to enjoy an intimate relationship, despite (or maybe because of) your pregnancy? When I ask this question of expectant mothers in my workshops, the responses range all over the map. Some women report that they're swinging from chandeliers, and others say that they've declared a moratorium on lovemaking.

Surprisingly, their answers have little to do with the quality of their relationships. Especially during pregnancy, sex isn't an accurate barometer of what's going on between two people. This is a time when some of the most loving couples make love the least.

Some men and women react strongly to the presence of the baby—the baby that literally comes between you and your mate when you have sex. You can't ignore it. You can't ask it to leave the room. So what *can* you do?

On the other hand, the baby's presence may *increase* your interest in lovemaking. It may enhance the tenderness and passion that you and your mate share during those times. Each act becomes a reaffirmation of the commitment you've made together.

Or you may feel protective of yourself and the baby. You, as the mother, and your baby are locked together in a sacred world for two, and you may not want to share that with your mate. Making love may seem like an invasion of your privacy.

Regardless of which description applies to you, sex during pregnancy is *different*. Unless conception marked your first intimate encounter, you and your mate had a sexual history. You established certain patterns and styles of lovemaking, and pregnancy has disrupted them. It may have altered the frequency, reassigned the roles (who initiates? who waits to be asked?), and necessitated finding more comfortable positions.

Sexuality is in the mind as well as the body. Emotionally, you may *both* be on shaky ground. Your mate may be overwhelmed by your ultrafeminine shape or genuinely frightened of the possibility of hurting the baby. Your new sense of fulfillment—and of being "filled up"—may be so strong that you find it hard to shift your attention away from the baby. You *and* your mate may be distracted by your excitement about and anticipation of the future.

No matter how you feel, it's important to acknowledge, examine, and talk about those feelings—especially if you're tending toward a protective, keep-out attitude. Even if you're still attracted to your mate, he may be getting the message that there isn't enough room for both him and the baby. And this can cause confusion and resentment.

If your interest in lovemaking has waned, don't keep the news locked inside. Talk to your mate. Ask hard questions. Use these for starters:

- Are you still attracted to me?
- Do you still like making love with me?
- How do you feel about our sexual relationship now?
- Is there anything you're scared of? If so, what?
- What do you want from our sexual relationship?

When you ask hard questions, you have to be willing to hear the answers. You may not like what you hear, but at least you'll be communicating. And that's a start.

Pregnancy is a time when the two of you are especially vulnerable to rejection. Silence, sarcasm, a turned-away shoulder, or jokes about extramarital affairs are no substitute for honest communication.

View this as an opportunity to clear up any misunderstandings that may exist between you. For example, you may have sensed that he isn't attracted to you anymore, and that's why he's holding back. Say so! He may reply that you're more gorgeous than ever, but he's been afraid of hurting the baby.

Or he may feel that three's a crowd. He should tell you! If he does, you'll have the chance to explain that you've been feeling clumsy and unattractive.

Unless you're both mind readers, asking—and answering—questions remains the best way to find out about each other. Learning something is almost always better than remaining in the dark, especially about matters as important as physical intimacy.

HIDDEN AGENDAS

Sex can be a silent language in which we express our innermost thoughts. You and your mate may be using it to communicate unspoken feelings. For example, you may be making love more than ever to prove that you haven't lost your appeal for each other. Meanwhile, you may be entertaining subconscious fears of losing him to another woman who isn't pregnant, and *he* may be afraid of losing his first-place position in your life.

What if you're making love less? Perhaps your pregnancy is serving as an excuse, a way out of having to confront uncomfortable truths. If either of you didn't enjoy sex before, or if you experienced it as an obligation or a nuisance, then you may view pregnancy as having gotten you off the hook. If your mate is withholding, it may be due to jealousy or resentment of your intimate bond with the baby. If there are other problems in your relationship, saying no to sex can be a subtle form of punishment. Or maybe you're both too tired or too stressed to bother.

Depending on how long the two of you have been together, you've probably already gone through a number of peaks and valleys in your sexual relationship. We all have times when we feel very sexual and times when our passion is at a low ebb (or nonexistent). These fluctuations can seem more threatening during pregnancy, especially if you wonder whether they contain hidden meanings.

If he's turned off by your pregnant body, you may imagine he'll also have a negative reaction to breast-feeding. If you're absorbed with the baby, he may wonder if he'll end up having to compete for your affection. And both of you may be terrified that pregnancy and parenthood signal the end to wonderfully wanton, whenever-you-want-it sex. (In some ways, they do.)

The patterns you form now will set the stage for your sexual relationship once the baby is born. It's not that mothers aren't sexy, or that taking care of children precludes passion. But if you plan to have a fulfilling sexual relationship in the future, don't wait until then to get serious about it. Particularly as your child gets older, you'll have to become even more flexible. Why not practice at this stage?

As it turns out, pregnancy is a useful and instructive prelude to parenthood. There are ample similarities between the two. At present, your attachment to the baby may make you less attentive to your mate. As a mother, there will be countless occasions when you'll be torn between their needs. But if you insist on *always* putting your child first, your love relationship will eventually erode.

The physical discomforts of pregnancy may be inhibiting your desire. Or maybe you're just not in the mood as often as you once were. Things won't necessarily get any easier once the baby is born. Coping with the frenzied pace of motherhood and a career isn't very conducive to feeling relaxed and responsive. Climbing out of bed for night feedings (or, later, to soothe night terrors) can call a halt to a cozy interlude. This may be your last chance for years to spend an entire Sunday lazing around together. Take it!

Most parents agree that it's difficult to sustain an active sexual relationship with a child around the house. It requires planning, motivation, and the ability to shift gears at a second's notice. At times, you'll have to shut out your other responsibilities mentally in order to concentrate on staying intimate with your mate. The challenge will be to balance your needs with the demands of parenthood.

Right now what you may need more than anything else is a sense of perspective—not to mention a sense of humor. At the moment, making love may seem more like a slapstick comedy than a steamy romance. Experimenting with new positions, or the sight of your skimpy camisole riding on top of your belly, may send you and your mate into gales of laughter long before you reach orgasm. Once the baby arrives, its insistence on crying three minutes into your foreplay may have the same effect. As long as you can laugh together, your relationship will survive.

Meanwhile, consider other forms of intimacy. There are countless alternatives to intercourse. Long walks, quiet talks, and evenings out can contribute to your feelings of closeness. Warm baths, back rubs, and snuggling can be pretty sexy all by themselves. Learning to touch each other in new ways can improve the quality of your lovemaking and deepen the bonds between you.

FOR FATHERS—*From Fathers*

NOTE: *Although I've spoken with many "pregnant" husbands and boyfriends, I think that the subject of male sexuality is best dealt with by men, so I asked some of the ones I know to share their thoughts and feelings. Here's what they had to say.*

Philip:

"You used to see her as a sexy tigress, and suddenly she's a madonna—inaccessible, even intimidating. In some ways, you're as attracted to her as before, but you're also confused.

"She's not behaving at all like her old self. First she doesn't want sex, then she wants more sex than ever, and then, when you do try to get passionate, the baby kicks and the whole thing seems ridiculous.

"What's a pregnant father to do?

"For me, it helped to admit that our sexual relationship had just been thrown a curve ball. I stopped expecting myself to feel the way I used to, and left myself open for new and different feelings. They were interesting, to say the least!"

Eric:

"When you first find out that your mate is pregnant, you'll probably be somewhat in awe of her body. You know there's something fragile inside it, something important going on. Even if both of you are still very interested in sex, you probably won't go at it with wild abandon. Everything you've read and heard says that you can't hurt the baby, but it seems impossible to ignore that tiny, growing presence.

"Once she's in the second trimester and out of the 'danger zone,' you'll probably feel more secure about making love. This is the period of pregnancy that will seem most like the old days. She'll have more energy, and you'll be more relaxed.

"Then, right about the time you're getting back into the swing of things, her body will start to change. You may find yourself missing the curve of her waist—which has disappeared—and you'll wonder whether sex is comfortable for her. On the other hand, you may enjoy some of the other changes in her body, like her bigger breasts and more voluptuous shape. And you may feel especially tender and close to her."

Jon:

"Sex during the third trimester requires a sense of humor. It doesn't seem to matter where you touch her anymore; the baby pops up everywhere. You can't escape the little kicks and jabs, and the thought of tiny feet and fists inches away (or closer) can be disconcerting.

"There's also the question of keeping your balance. None of your favorite positions works anymore. If your repertoire only includes one approach, you have to be more inventive. It also helps to be playful about it."

Alan:

"Sex late in pregnancy requires an extra effort, but it's also extra worthwhile. If this is your first baby, you should probably acknowledge that the honeymoon will soon be over for real. You can't make love for up to six weeks after the baby arrives.

"If you're already a father, you should try to savor this time. As you know, the next several months will be hectic."

Terry:

"If you're turned on by earth mother types, sex during pregnancy can be a peak experience. Then again, you may be one of those men who aren't the least bit interested in women with bellies the size of Volkswagens. In either case, it doesn't last forever. You'll be back to two in the bed before too long. Just be patient!"

Mike:

"Sex during pregnancy presents a whole new set of challenges. Some of these may be awkward or uncomfortable, but if the two of you keep talking, you may discover a fresh regard and respect for each other's bodies.

"If you're attracted to the way she looks, tell her! If you're not, that's okay, too—just don't be quite as verbal about it. If you're as sexually interested in her as ever, enjoy! If not, don't be hard on yourself. Feelings of uncertainty are perfectly normal, given the changes in her body and your relationship. Be supportive, but also be aware of your own emotional needs. You have every right to your feelings, and it's important to be honest with yourself and your mate."

FOR FATHERS—*From a Mother*

Honesty is a virtue, but so are sensitivity and tact. Right now your mate needs your approval. She's so aware of her body that she'll take anything you say about it to heart, so don't be careless.

There are many different ways to say the same thing. Think before you speak! And some things are better left unsaid. Certain words and phrases are buzz words to pregnant women, and they can have devastating effects. Expressions like "beached whale," "cow," and "fatso" are best eliminated from your vocabulary. You may think they're funny, but *she* won't.

The following list of do's and don'ts is offered strictly from a female point of view:

DO tell her what you like about her body.
    DON'T say, "You look okay, I guess."
DO let her know if you're afraid of hurting the baby.
    DON'T stop touching her.
DO comment on how her body is changing.
    DON'T act as if you haven't noticed.
DO listen when she says, "I look like a truck!"
    DON'T laugh.
DO put your hand on her belly to feel the baby move.
    DON'T fall asleep while you're doing it.
DO remember to tell her you love her—often.

Stage Three

9

Facing Your Fears

"Do you ever worry that something will be wrong with your baby?" I asked a pregnant friend of mine.

"Of course not," she replied. "I'm sure it will have twelve fingers and twelve toes."

We can joke about . . . we can ignore it . . . we can rationalize it. But the fact remains that for every pregnant woman, *fear is real*. It's present somewhere in our thoughts, dreams, and fantasies. And it seems to grow, like a shadow at dusk, the closer we get to childbirth.

It isn't easy to face our fears. It's natural to want to run away from the things that frighten us. We worry that if we stop and look closely at them, it will be like opening Pandora's box: Horrible things will jump out at us, things we can't control.

Writing this chapter meant looking back at fears I'd been glad to forget. Fears about false labor. Fears about making a fool of myself during labor—of looking awful, of losing control and screaming at Gary. Fears about having a baby that no one would think was beautiful.

I had other, deeper fears, but these I buried beneath layers of superficial anxiety. In one sense, I never really believed that my babies would be anything but perfect. Whenever I let my guard down, though, I heard a tiny, nagging voice in the back of my mind: *What about your lousy diet and all the coffee you drink? What about your crazy Aunt Marge on your father's side? What about your sister's friend's son, who was four months premature and still can't walk?* All around me was proof that the impossible *could* happen.

Maybe you've been facing your fears from the beginning. If so, congratulations; you're braver than most people. If not, now is the time.

FOUR REASONS TO FACE YOUR FEARS

You know from experience that there are certain things you have to come to terms with sooner or later, like a major disagreement with your mate, an unpleasant situation at work, or a misunderstanding with a close friend. If you don't, they are blown out of proportion and become even harder to deal with.

It's the same with your fears about childbirth and motherhood. Today, tomorrow, or the day after, you're going to have to face them—not to scare yourself silly, but to give yourself power over them. Let's look at how this works.

1. *Facing your fears makes them less frightening and more manageable.* A vivid imagination is a great gift—in almost any circumstance other than pregnancy. When we let our imaginations color our fears, a twig rubbing against the outside of the house can turn into a monster trying to get in. We can shake under the covers until morning comes, or we can go outside and discover the true source of the noise.

   Our worst fears are almost always unfounded. But we can't know that until we look at them and see them for what they really are.

2. *Facing your fears makes it possible to do something*

about them. Once we know that the noise is just a twig, we can choose to ignore the noise or to break the twig off the tree. *We* have control.

Are you worried that your medical provider will be on vacation when you go into labor? Ask about his or her plans for that time. If it looks chancy, arrange for a backup, someone else in the office you trust.

Are you afraid of going into the hospital? Arrange to take a tour that includes a look at a typical labor room and delivery room. See for yourself. Ask questions about things you don't understand.

3. *Facing your fears can reveal other areas in your life that need attention.* Are you frightened of the medical procedures involved in childbirth? Maybe you haven't chosen a doctor or midwife you trust or respect. Or maybe you haven't worked at building a good relationship with that person.

   Are you afraid that your mate won't be supportive during the birth? Maybe you need to encourage him to educate and prepare himself.

4. *Facing your fears can reveal their positive side.* The very fact that you have fears indicates that you've already developed a sense of responsibility about your baby. You're afraid for it because you care about it. You're scared of the childbirth experience because you want your child to have a safe journey and the best possible start in life.

   Your fears have a positive side. They're the first steps toward motherhood. They're proof that you're getting ready for your new role, and they predict the many years of commitment you'll make to your child's health and happiness.

What are you *most* afraid of? Which of the following words or phrases describes your deepest fear?

> PAIN . . . BIRTH DEFECTS . . . CESAREAN . . .
> PREMATURE LABOR . . . INDUCED LABOR . . . FORCEPS
> . . . DEFORMITIES . . . HYSTERIA . . . DEATH

Part of facing your fears involves expressing them—to your mate, to your medical provider, to your friends: people who will listen sympathetically and supportively.

But first you have to express them to *yourself*. Get started with this simple exercise: Go back and reread that list of scary words and phrases. Now read them *aloud* to yourself. And again.

Women who do this report surprising results: The more often they say these words and phrases, the less scary they become.

Most of the fears pregnant women have fall into two categories: fears about the baby (will it be okay?) and fears about the birth (will I be okay?). Let's explore each of these.

FEARS ABOUT THE BABY

At some point, *all* pregnant women wonder if their babies will be healthy and whole. We force ourselves to imagine the worst possibility, just in case. We read the statistics with morbid fascination and vacillate between confidence and doubt. "All the babies I know are healthy, and there's no reason mine should be any different." (Sigh of relief.) "Then again, maybe that means that my odds have worsened and I'm next in line to be one of the unlucky ones." (Panic!)

The number-one fear among pregnant women is that their babies will be born with severe defects or abnormalities. None of us can bear the thought of a child suffering years of hardship and pain, and the emotional and economic resources required are staggering. We worry about our abilities to look at, love, and live with such a child, and we prepare to blame ourselves for whatever went wrong.

The fear of having a stillborn baby is either less common or less talked about. Particularly for first-time mothers, the idea of carrying a child to full term and then losing it is beyond the bounds of imagination. And for some people, it may be easier to accept the idea of a stillborn baby than one with serious problems. They may feel that stillbirth is unquestionably a fluke of nature, a cosmic mistake that could not have been avoided and therefore brings less guilt.

Women who have had a difficult time conceiving, women over age thirty-five, and women who are already mothers are more likely to fixate on this latter scenario. In the first two instances, a sense of lost time—of having worked so hard or waited so long to have a child—results in an increased investment in its survival. Women pregnant with their second (or third, or tenth) child know how precious children are and have a very real sense of how terrible it would be to lose one.

We hesitate to talk about our fear of losing the baby or of having a deformed child. It's too morbid to discuss; other people might ridicule us. Even if we're not superstitious, we can't help wondering if such talk could be a self-fulfilling prophecy.

If we do voice our fears, people tell us that in this day and age, severe birth defects are too rare even to think about. From a purely mathematical perspective, they're right; 98 percent of the babies born in the United States today are healthy. Why dwell on something that is so unlikely to happen?

But birth defects do happen, and not always to strangers. Sometimes it happens to people we know and love.

Nancy was thirty-four when she became pregnant for the first time. "Everything was going smoothly, and then one day I walked into work and found the office strangely quiet," she recalls. "The normal chatter was absent, and people were going about their business looking as if we were all about to be fired. I asked someone what was going on.

"Then I heard that a co-worker's baby had been born with spina bifida. I took the morning off and rushed to the library to read every article written about the disease. If it could happen to her, it could happen to me. That baby stayed on my mind throughout the rest of my pregnancy."

Fortunately, medical technology has advanced to a stage at which ultrasound, amniocentesis, and fetal monitors can accurately diagnose many severe problems long before birth. State-of-the-art neonatal programs keep babies alive who would not have had a chance until recently.

Less than a century ago, however, the perfect baby was more the exception than the rule. Many of our grandmothers had still-born children. I was shocked to learn that my Grandma Sophie would have had six more brothers and sisters had they survived.

Your fears about your baby may be symbolic of other, less obvious fears you're having. Worries about whether it will be healthy may reflect your concerns about assuming responsibility for it once it's born. Or they may signify some anxiety or guilt you're feeling about your prenatal diet or use of medications. The media are full of warnings about smoking, drinking, and drugs during pregnancy. What if something happens that could have been prevented?

Visions of losing the baby (or your own life) may also be connected to the very real losses we incur in the passage from pregnancy to motherhood. Childbirth is both a beginning and an end, a hello and a good-bye. The moment your baby leaves your body, it no longer belongs exclusively to you. And your old familiar life is gone forever, replaced with parenthood. You may fear losing your freedom, your youth, and the certainties of your past.

Finally, you may fear a whole host of unknowns. While you're eager to get to know your child, you may also be afraid of meeting him or her in the flesh. Will your baby be healthy and easy to care for? Will you experience love at first sight, or will it take time to become attached to your child? Will motherhood come naturally or be a struggle?

You can't begin to answer any of these questions now. Consider them part of the great mystery of birth!

Earlier we talked about the importance of facing your fears. Here are some ways to fight your fears about the baby:

- Don't dwell on morbid scenarios. It's natural to feel some trepidation, but focus instead on the far more likely possibility that your baby will be alive and well.
- Talk to your baby *in utero;* many women do. It can help you to affirm your baby's presence. Also try singing, stroking your tummy, or drawing funny faces on it. (Okay, so you'll look funny to outsiders. Who cares?)
- Think good thoughts about the baby, about yourself, about your mate, about the three of you together as a family. You'll be sending your child positive psychic messages.

- Ask your medical provider about the possibility of scheduling an ultrasound. Seeing your baby is one way to ease your fears.

Unexpected Endings

Everyone prays for a perfect baby, but we live in an imperfect world. Although we're capable of sending people to the moon, we still have a lot to learn about the nature of human life.

Tragedies do happen. We can be thankful they don't happen often. When they do, however, they permanently alter the lives of everyone involved.

Nothing compares to the loss one experiences when one has a dead or deformed baby, but the stages of grief are similar to those one goes through when experiencing any other significant loss.[1]

The first reaction is usually disbelief. If you should learn that there's something wrong with your baby, you may feel numb or even go into shock. If the baby is in trouble and immediate decisions are necessary, you may find it hard to assimilate information and make educated choices.

That's why you should try to consider this possibility ahead of time, even though it will be very painful. Long before my due dates, my husband and I discussed with our doctor what we would do if we were faced with the either/or of life-sustaining devices versus death at our own request. You may want to call on a friend, a family member, or your spiritual adviser to help you through these difficult issues.

Your next reaction is likely to be anger or rage. "How could this happen to me? What did I do to deserve it?" You may direct your anger toward anyone in sight, including your mate, your doctor, or the hospital personnel. It's natural to look for someone to blame at a time like this. Such anger is appropriate and part of the healing process, and it's essential to express it, even if it means flailing around or losing control. The sooner you let it out of your system, the easier it will be to let it go altogether.

Beneath your rage will be tears of sadness, disappointment, and pain. If your baby is born with severe birth defects, you may feel deep sadness for the lifelong hardships that you both will endure. You will worry about how you will care for it in the months and years to come.

If your baby is stillborn, you will grieve for a loss that is greater than any other imaginable. For a while you may feel as if you have no feelings left.

As improbable as this seems, the pain will lessen and fade over time. But you will always feel a certain emptiness inside, a memory of what you lost and can never regain.

Eventually you will reach a place of acceptance. What happened cannot be reversed, but we all have the capacity for coming to terms with the most catastrophic situations.

Part of acceptance involves facing the truth. If your baby is born with a birth defect or disability, there is much you will have to learn about the child's condition and its special needs. You will need to talk to other parents who have had similar experiences.

If your child is stillborn, I highly recommend that you insist on holding it, naming it, and going through a ritual burial that will formally express your sorrow.

You will feel isolated. You will feel as if nothing this terrible has ever happened to anyone but you. In a very real sense, you will be right.

You may want to avoid those of your friends who have healthy children, and you may find that even the most well meaning people say the wrong things. Parents of a stillborn child report that friends and family assume it is inappropriate even to mention the child. Yet these parents hold their lost child in their hearts, and that baby remains every bit as real as the children born before and after.

Finally, you will forgive yourself. In the words of Rabbi Harold Kushner, "Bad things happen to good people."[2] Although you will search your memory for things you might have done differently to avoid this sad outcome, you will probably end up with more questions than answers.

The truth is, *these things just happen.* And when they do, we usually find that we have the extra something it takes to rise above a difficult challenge. The most trying experiences in life provide the greatest opportunities for personal growth, since they demand courage, commitment, and belief in oneself.

If you are one of those special individuals and you have returned to this book in the hope of finding some comfort, I offer you this promise: You will regain your strength and survive your experience—not with bitterness, but with wisdom.

FEARS ABOUT THE BIRTH

We anticipate childbirth with equal portions of excitement and trepidation. We can hardly wait for labor to begin, yet we're fearful of what it will be like.

Childbirth is scary because it's an unknown. No matter how much you read about it, prepare for it, and talk to other women about it, it *remains* an unknown.

Over the years, you may have heard your mother or grandmother talk about childbirth, euphemistically and in a hushed tone. Your friends may go into detail about their experiences, but everyone forgets to mention the one thing you're most anxious to know: *How does it feel?*

Childbirth education has come a long way in the past twenty years. In the United States, 65 percent of all pregnant women attend childbirth education classes,[3] with most signing up during their first trimester.

These classes are helpful in many ways. They teach us the medical terminology we need to know and instruct us in breathing and relaxation techniques. They legitimize the notion that childbirth is an important experience, one that should be approached with knowledge and careful preparation. They draw our mates into the pregnancy by assigning them the title of "coach" and an active and important role in the birth process.

Basically, they give us what we want: We want to interact with other pregnant couples, and we want to know how to go through childbirth safely and successfully. Of necessity, that means focusing on the specifics of labor and delivery. For many couples, learning about contractions and picturing themselves as the laboring couple in the film can be sobering and scary. Childbirth classes present the realities, sometimes without taking into account the sensitive nature of the material. They may fall short by neglecting to focus on the *emotional* aspects of getting ready for childbirth.

They do an excellent job of readying the mind and the body. They may ignore one essential source of strength: the spirit.

Childbirth is one of the most traumatic and demanding events in a woman's life. It requires enormous stamina, and it takes everything you've got—including determination, vision, commitment, and courage.

The three most common fears women have about childbirth are *the fear of pain, the fear of losing control,* and *performance anxiety.* Coping with these requires spiritual tools, not just physical ones. Let's look closely at each.

The Fear of Pain

There are very few, if any, women who aren't apprehensive about the pain of childbirth. Women who have had babies hesitate to mention the word "pain," and childbirth educators may talk instead about "pressure." But we have all heard, somewhere along the line, that *having a baby hurts.*

Diana didn't realize that she had dilated to 10 centimeters until her midwife told her. "I went right through transition without even knowing it," she says. "I felt a slight cramping—less than my normal menstrual cramps. My baby was born within twenty minutes." So apparently there *is* such a thing as painless childbirth.

For most women, though, it isn't that easy. We've all heard women use such expressions as "climbing the walls," and we're aware that not too long ago, most women were put to sleep during childbirth. Our expectation and anticipation of pain is constantly reinforced.

My own mother tells me that she actually tried to escape from the delivery table. The last thing she remembered was the oxygen mask coming down over her face.

If labor hurt too much for our mothers to stay conscious, how can we possibly stand it?

Another reason we worry about the pain of childbirth is that we have nothing to compare it to. Not knowing what it's like, we have no way to prepare ourselves.

Some women say that labor is like a severe menstrual period. Others compare it to portaging a canoe uphill while having a root canal performed. (Joan Rivers claims that it's like taking hold of your upper lip and pulling it over the top of your head!) Still others are at a loss for words.

So we have to fill in the blanks. We usually call upon our past experiences of pain and try to imagine the sensation of contractions.

Jan's strongest memories of pain go back to her childhood, when she fell out of a tree and broke her leg. Kelly has migraine headaches and thinks that's what labor must feel like. Women who have had abortions often imagine that labor will feel much the same.

What we hear about pushing is equally confusing. Some women find it pleasurable and even compare it to having an orgasm. Others feel as if their bodies are splitting in half in an excruciating tug-of-war between themselves and all the forces of nature.

It makes sense to worry about pain during labor and delivery when we can't get an exact description of it. Unfortunately, we'll probably *never* get such a description—or any kind of consensus.

That's because childbirth is a highly subjective experience. Every labor progresses at its own pace and intensity. Every woman has a different pain threshold, and every baby emerges in its own fashion. How can you possibly describe something that only happens once?

There's yet another reason for the vagueness associated with descriptions of childbirth: the loss-of-memory syndrome. Women often say that they *can't remember* what it feels like.

Their memories start fading just moments after giving birth. Kate forgot what her contractions felt like as she passed from one to the next—and they were thirty seconds apart!

What causes the loss-of-memory syndrome? The sheer excitement of finally seeing the baby? Do we deliberately block out our feelings or discard them? Have we been taught to submerge the graphic details of labor and delivery?

We'd all be less afraid of pain if we had some firsthand information to hold on to. Perhaps every woman should make the commitment to memorize her childbirth experience so she can someday pass it on to her daughter. I can still recall both of mine, vividly and down to the last detail. They're permanently frozen in my memory because I *decided* not to forget. I worked hard to bring my children into the world, and what happened is worth remembering.

The Fear of Losing Control

Most women fear losing control in one or both of two ways: They're afraid of having to abdicate their power, and they're worried about becoming hysterical.

We fear that others will make the decisions at a time when we most want to be in charge. The fact that the majority of births take place in modern hospitals doesn't help. The lack of familiarity with our surroundings, and the high-tech environment common to most hospitals, aren't at all encouraging. Our fear is intensified by images of sterile, white hallways and sharp steel instruments.

Will the natural flow of labor and delivery be interrupted by forced medication or unwanted intervention? Will your hopes for birthing in complete awareness be diminished by the need for a cesarean?

As a veteran of two hospital births, I'm grateful for the excellent medical care and attention I received. They proved especially critical during my daughter's birth. The stirrups that had looked so menacing during my hospital tour turned out to be a big help when I had to push. The one pain shot I asked for gave me a second wind when I needed it. The umbilical cord was wrapped around the baby's neck, and forceps were required. Immediate attention averted what might have been a dangerous situation.

Yet I'm still counting my losses from that experience. I spent most of my thirty-four hours of labor lying flat on my back, connected to monitors and stripped of my power. After four hours of pushing, I had to let the doctor pull my daughter from my womb. I did not see her born, and I will always regret it.

So there's some sacrifice involved in taking advantage of the latest medical technology. We want safety, but we also want the final say. Often we end up forgoing the latter.

Events can happen quickly, and the best-laid plans can go awry. But there *are* some things you can do to retain at least a portion of your power while giving birth in a hospital:

- Unless your circumstances are extraordinary, there's no reason you should have to be totally unconscious. (It's even possible to be awake during a cesarean.) Well in advance of your due date, ask your doctor to describe the various drugs and their effects. Voice your preferences.
- Ask questions during labor and delivery. Find out what's being done to you and why. Most nurses and doctors will be glad to explain.
- Although it's not always possible, you should be able to exercise some say over who is in the labor or delivery room with you. You don't have to be the main attraction on a medical students' tour.
- Make sure that your mate knows your wants and wishes. Two voices are stronger than one.
- If there's something you object to, speak up!
- Keep in mind that the doctors and nurses are there to help you. Your styles may be different, but you all have the same goal: getting your baby born safely.

Now let's talk about "freaking out." Translation: "losing it," "losing your cool," or, to put it in plain English, "making a complete and total fool of yourself right in front of everybody."

We all worry about this. Although we *know* it doesn't matter how we behave during labor and delivery (after all, stars are expected to be temperamental), we still want to act and look our best.

But other stars have opportunities to rehearse for their performance before going on. They have private dressing rooms and plenty of chances to freshen their makeup.

Labor can start at any time. And once it does, you're on—ready or not!

If you deliver your baby in a hospital, you will have little or no privacy during childbirth. Many women find this particularly hard to take. They may have gotten used to their medical providers staring at and poking around their private parts, but the thought of strangers doing it is another matter. Nurses, other doctors, technicians, and aides may all wander in and out of your room.

You may be worried about losing your temper, your dinner, your manners, or your modesty. You may wonder whether you'll involuntarily make animal-like noises or soil the bed—distinctly "unladylike" behaviors we're deeply conditioned against. You may be apprehensive about the whole earthy, public nature of childbirth—and for good reason. Your genitals will be exposed and your bodily functions will be openly discussed.

Childbirth leaves us naked to the world. It tosses our sexual inhibitions and good manners out the window. So-called breeding, background, education, and social position become irrelevant; the process of giving birth is the same for peasants and princesses. We're *all* subject to it—and we're *all* elevated by it. It's something only women can do, and it's one thing that makes us special.

Although you may find this difficult to believe until after you've experienced childbirth, *your behavior during it won't matter*. You won't care about how your hair looks or whether you swear at your doctor. Your *only* concern will be that of giving birth to your child.

Lucy, a normally modest and decorous individual, put it this way: "They could have wheeled me into a shopping mall stark naked. They could have hauled me into Congress with my gown up around my neck. They could have put me on the nightly news before an audience of millions. I wouldn't have noticed, and I wouldn't have cared. I was busy with something more important —having my baby."

Performance Anxiety

We all go into childbirth determined to do a "good job." We want our mate and medical provider to be proud of us. We want to come through with flying colors—not fall flat on our faces.

I was all set to be Sarah Bernhardt, the star of the sold-out performance. Glistening with sweat beneath the spotlight of opening night, I would bear my child to roars of applause. My birth would be the best show that anyone had ever seen.

Sometimes, as we prepare for the great event, we forget the real goal of childbirth: bringing the baby safely into the world. We focus too much on ourselves. The classes we attend and the books we read don't help; many of them give the false impression that there's a "right" way and a "wrong" way to give birth. There's no way to fail, yet we struggle to succeed as if the Oscar for Best Actress were at stake.

Every mother who successfully goes through labor and delivery deserves an A plus. *Every* performance is the best possible performance.

To repeat: once you're in the midst of it, *you won't care.*

Taking Charge—and Letting Go

Interestingly, most of the fears we have about childbirth disappear the moment we go into labor. It's then that our true priorities assert themselves.

Nevertheless, these fears can plague us for the nine months leading up to the Great Event. And that's why they're worth doing something about.

In Chapter 4, I talked about the paradox of *taking charge* and *letting go*—two seemingly contradictory acts that actually complement each other. There I applied them to pregnancy, but they're just as useful for countering the fears associated with childbirth.

TAKING CHARGE

1. *Go into childbirth prepared* to assert your power and stay on top of the situation. You may want to practice relaxation techniques, breathing exercises, or even self-hypnosis as a way of altering the way you experience pain.
2. *Get all the information you can.* As discussed before, it can be reassuring to visit the hospital ahead of time and take a look around. Learn about the medical procedures involved in childbirth. Familiarize yourself with the terminology your doctor will be using.
3. *Make your preferences known ahead of time.* Discuss them openly and thoroughly with both your mate and your medical provider. Be sure that *everyone* knows how *you* want things to go.

    Julie developed a detailed birth plan specifying her choices regarding medication and other types of intervention. In it she wrote, "If I ask for pain medication, the nurses are to wait fifteen minutes in case I change my mind."
4. *Create a positive image of yourself giving birth.* Envision yourself as strong and powerful. See yourself as assertive and deserving of respect.

Prepare for a positive birth experience and commit yourself to having it.

LETTING GO

1. *Be willing to alter your expectations of the birth.* No matter how many preparations you make in advance, you may have to change your expectations when reality presents itself.

    Let's say you've planned for an unmedicated birth. But

what if you feel different once you're in labor? Or you've been determined to stay at home until you've dilated to 5 centimeters. But what if you arrive at the hospital, find out that it's false labor, and have to turn around and go back? Or you've promised yourself to spend much of your labor moving around. But what if a fetal monitor becomes a safety measure instead of a choice? Or you've pictured yourself pushing your baby out and instantly nursing. But what if a cesarean means the difference between life and death?

You can hope and plan all you want, but real life holds no guarantees. Don't paint yourself into a corner.

Stacey had always longed to have a home birth, with a midwife attending and her friends gathered around. When an ultrasound revealed placenta previa, she was forced to rethink her plans. She found a doctor who promised to cooperate with her midwife at the hospital and take over only in the event of an emergency. She compromised her preference for the sake of her baby's safety.

2. *Be willing to alter your expectations of yourself.* Childbirth is an opportunity to forget your inhibitions and scream like a banshee, if that's what you feel like doing. Other people will forgive you if you lose your cool or shriek at the nurses. No one expects you to act like a lady when you're giving birth.

In the end, I was no Sarah Bernhardt. I whimpered, cried, and begged for medication when I couldn't stand it any longer. But I gave birth, and that's what counts.

3. *Avoid taking responsibility for anyone else's experience.* You may also be concerned about helping your mate feel comfortable during the birth. While it's natural to want him to have a positive experience too, don't get carried away. A woman once told me that she was worried about whether her husband would have a good time. This is going too far.

During childbirth, *you're* the one who matters most, and the last thing you need to do is take care of someone else. You're busy birthing the baby, and that's more than enough.

4. *Be prepared to relinquish your desire to control.* Tradi-

tional childbirth education teaches that it's possible to "manage" the pain of contractions. Maybe; maybe not. The disadvantage to this approach is that it leaves us no other choice. We feel as if we *must* breathe and count, breathe and count, as if we *must* stay in control of something that's primarily out of our hands. Actually dealing with contractions requires a fine balancing act of staying in charge and letting your body take over.

5. *Let others do their jobs.* It's okay to ask questions and voice any objections you may have, but the truth is that the professionals around you will know things you don't. Give them room to take care of your medical needs and those of the baby.

6. *Have faith.* Letting go means placing your trust in the things you can be sure of—yourself, your body, and the baby.

You're doing a terrific job carrying your child. Why should you doubt your ability to give it birth?

When the first contraction comes, labor will begin. Your body will know its cue—just as the sun knows how to rise even if the rooster doesn't crow.

Your baby will know when it's time, and it will find a way to be born. Trust its capacity to complete the journey.

If you've chosen your medical provider carefully, and if you've been honest with your mate about your expectations and needs, you can trust them, too. They'll come through for you and provide you with the best care they're capable of giving.

Give yourself permission to let go, and you'll be more relaxed and able to appreciate the spontaneity of birth.

FEAR AND POWER

When we're afraid, we feel helpless. Our muscles involuntarily tense, and adrenaline races through our bodies. It seems as if we're shrinking in size, like Alice in Wonderland.

How do you experience fear? Everyone reacts differently when faced with something frightening. Some people become paralyzed, while others snap into action. Your responses may be rooted in your childhood, when you were more vulnerable and less able to protect yourself. Or maybe you were the kid on the block who always took the risks.

Do you ever invite fear by going to a scary movie, just for the fun of it? Or is fear the enemy, something to be shunned? Some people thrive on tense situations, viewing them as opportunities to sharpen their skills and muster their wits and bravado. Others go out of their way to avoid fear.

Your fears are a natural response to the unknowns of childbirth. You cannot do away with them altogether, but you can diminish them, *for power is just as real as fear.*

You *can* counteract your feelings of helplessness and master your fears. But this takes more than the physical tools of prepared childbirth. It also takes the emotional tools of spiritual power.

Childbirth is a powerful experience, and going through it requires power. Over the past few months, your power has been growing. You've learned about nutrition, relaxation techniques, and the medical procedures involved in birth. You've gained a greater regard for your body's strength, and you've developed a protective bond with your child. You're rested, relaxed, and ready for what lies ahead—your own unique experience of bringing your child into the world.

That experience may push you to the limit. What will you do? Although you can't really know until you're there, you can begin to get a sense of your power and inner resources. Perhaps you've already tapped into yours many times, whenever you've encountered a situation that required extra physical or emotional energy —like running a race, completing a difficult task, or caring for someone in need.

As women, we tend to be shy about our power or even to deny it. We've been taught to be humble, to downplay our strength, to dismiss our accomplishments as luck. We hesitate to advertise our own strengths because we don't want others to think we're immodest or conceited. But being conceited is having an excessively high opinion of oneself; being aware of your power is simply knowing who you are and what you're made of.

It's important to realize and appreciate the extent of your personal power, both as you go through childbirth and as you deal with other challenges in your life. Think back. Remember how it felt to acknowledge and use your own strength and courage. It may have been something simple, like getting through an illness or speaking up for yourself. Or it may have been something more dramatic, like saving someone's life.

What happened when you were pushed to the limit?

Every story of personal courage culminates in a moment of truth. At that point, people make a conscious choice to move beyond their fear and do whatever they have to do.

The same is true for the experience of childbirth. Approach it with a sense of your personal power, and you'll leave your fears behind. You'll still feel the contractions, you may need intervention, but you'll feel like a victor, not a victim.

Childbirth can be an opportunity for spiritual growth. Your body will work harder than it has ever worked before, and your spirit will be stretched every bit as much. Reach inside to the source of your power, and you'll give birth to yourself as well as your baby.

FEAR THAT THE BABY WON'T COME

You've cleaned the house, arranged the nursery, and packed and unpacked for the seventeenth time. The forty-week mark is looming, and your medical provider has penciled in one more appointment just in case. Starting maternity leave early seemed like a good idea last August. So did your mother's supersaver airline tickets, which are about to expire. And if one more person says, "When's the big day?" you might not be able to be polite. In short, you've had enough. So where's the baby?

Nine months is a long time to wait, and those last few weeks can seem like a lifetime. Whether we admit it or not, most women think their due dates are as certain as a national holiday; they forget that it's a statistical prediction with two weeks leeway on either side. Only 4 percent of babies are born exactly on their estimated due date, yet we secretly hope to be one of the lucky ones who go early (not too early) or right on time, and we're disappointed if the day comes and goes without the long-awaited first contraction that our lives seem to hinge on. Never before have we waited so eagerly for the onset of pain.

The ninth month is especially difficult for a variety of reasons. As the due date draws near for first-time mothers, the suspense is mixed with anxiety about how to recognize a real contraction and when to make an appearance at the hospital. Veteran mothers have the added stress of detailed planning: Will the birth coincide with prearranged plans for their other children?

Around this time, more experienced friends may urge you to take advantage of your soon-to-be-diminished freedom. But sitting in a movie for two hours or staying up late for a romantic tryst is easier said than done. While you have probably seen other women at full term, you probably never imagined you could be so large. The accompanying physical discomforts and frequent trips to the bathroom may limit your mobility as well as your motivation to go out. As the old saying goes, your get up and go may have got up and left.

The famous "nesting urge" is one way that women cope with waiting—using the time to finish last-minute projects. Other women savor this period as a chance to reflect on the pregnancy and replenish their resources. Many women begin their maternity leave a few weeks prior to the due date. This can be a wonderful opportunity to rest and prepare for the baby. On the other hand, removing yourself from the stimulation of the office can result in boredom and increased anxiety. An ideal solution might be to arrange a flexible schedule, gradually reducing the work load. But some women prefer to work right up to the last minute.

A local television newscaster went into labor during the six o'clock news and finished the broadcast before heading for the hospital. Everyone in Minneapolis followed her pregnancy all the way to the recovery room. Most pregnancies don't elicit quite that much attention, but in the last few days, it may seem as if everyone you know is on pins and needles waiting for the birth. Friends start calling, co-workers joke about delivering in the elevator, and your mate takes notice every time a funny expression crosses your face. You may welcome the attention or it may begin to feel like pressure, especially if the baby is late. After a while, you may even begin to feel apologetic, as if somehow you're responsible for not delivering on deadline.

Zoe was two weeks late, and during the first week, friends called constantly to see if I was still at home. By the second week, the phone would ring, I'd answer, there would be a short pause, and the caller would hang up. Apparently hearing my voice was the answer to the caller's question.

If possible, try not to feel pressured by other people's queries. Most likely they are simply excited about the baby and want to be kept up on all the details. However, if their curiosity becomes a problem, let people know that you will call when the baby comes, and if all else fails, take your phone off the hook.

If your pregnancy has been normal up to this point, there is no medical basis for concern if you are two weeks "late." Neither the baby's health nor your chances of having a straightforward delivery are jeopardized. Still, it is natural to worry about what will happen if the pregnancy goes on too long. Many women fear that they will have to be induced if labor doesn't begin spontaneously, ruining their hopes for a more natural birth experience. These fears are easily intensified when your thoughts are monopolized by labor and delivery.

Ultimately, the only choice is to wait. While you have lots of control over other areas of your pregnancy, unless you are scheduled to be induced or to have a cesarean, the baby's time of arrival is strictly out of your control. As advanced as medicine is, doctors have yet to discover what causes the onset of labor. The unknown is both magical and frustrating.

YOUR BEST IS ENOUGH

You've done everything possible to smooth the way for the Perfect Birth Experience. You've taken childbirth education classes, you've drawn up a birth plan, you've gotten your mate interested and involved, you've asserted your needs, and you're prepared to bring your personal power with you into the labor room.

But what if things don't work out according to plan? What if childbirth falls short of your hopes and dreams? How will you feel about yourself?

We all begin the experience wanting and expecting it to proceed a certain way. If it doesn't, we're likely to feel disappointed, angry, or ashamed. We may allow our regret to overshadow our joy.

And that's too bad—because there's no reason for it. During childbirth, *your best is enough*. Right now you care very much about the way in which you'll give birth. In twenty years or so, when you're sharing the story with your daughter or son, they won't care that you called their father names or kicked the doctor. Instead, they'll focus on the miracle and magic of being there because of what you did. As Claudia Panuthos wrote in her book *Transformation Through Birth*, "Angels can do no better."[4]

FOR COACHES

Childbirth is your big chance to *really* come through for the woman you love. It's a demanding, often painful process, and your mate will need all the support and encouragement you can give. Over the several hours it will probably take, her feelings will fluctuate between confidence and fear, apprehension and hope. Sometimes she may even think that she isn't going to make it. You'll have your work cut out for you!

To prepare for your part as coach, try to imagine yourself at the birth. Project your feelings and responses. Then, when the time comes, keep these things in mind:

- *Your presence matters.* In fact, you're probably the *most* important person in the room as far as your mate is concerned. She's depending on you to be there for her, no matter what happens. The medical personnel are supervising the birth; you're participating in it.

- *You know what you're doing—and you can help.* You've been through childbirth education classes, and you know how to make your mate feel more comfortable and relaxed. Use the skills you've learned.

- *You are her advocate.* She expects you to serve as liaison between her and the medical professionals, to negotiate on her behalf for the things she wants and needs. She's busy giving birth. It's your responsibility to see that, within the limits of safety, the actual experience comes as close as possible to being the way she planned it.

- *Her pain is not your fault.* You certainly played your part in conceiving the child, but *she wanted this baby too,* even if she denies it in the middle of a contraction. Pain is integral to childbirth. It's not easy to watch, but it won't last forever.

- *Don't take it personally if she loses her temper.* Women in labor are known for saying terrible things they don't mean. Remember that your mate is under a great deal of stress. Even if she appears to be spoiling for a fight, swallow your pride and avoid it. Besides, she's not angry at you, only at her own feelings of helplessness.

- *Your feelings are appropriate and valid.* Fear, anxiety, insecurity, guilt, powerlessness—you may be feeling a whole range of emotions. Almost everyone in your position does. Acknowledge them, but don't let them get in the way. Your mate, not your feelings, should take center stage.

- *You were chosen.* Your mate chose *you* to be her coach. Why? Because she would rather have you at her birth than anyone else in the world.

Men who have attended the births of their children describe it as a life-changing and awesome experience. They feel closer to their children, they respect women more, and they often come away with a new and profound appreciation of life.

One thing is certain: It's an experience you'll *never* forget.

Stage Four

10

POSTPARTUM:
The Bridge

"Postpartum" refers to the period after delivery—the bridge between pregnancy and motherhood—and most of us approach it with dread. We're excited to learn that we're pregnant, and we look forward to raising our children, but we don't anticipate the passage with pleasure. It's like going to the dentist with a toothache: You know you have to do it, but you wish you didn't.

We envision sleepless nights and screaming babies, crying jags and attacks of the dreaded "postpartum blues." Our friends warn us to "get all the rest you can now—you'll need it!" Women have told me that their husbands thought they were going crazy.

The postpartum stage *does* come as a shock. While the changes of pregnancy occur gradually and motherhood is yours for life, postpartum happens instantaneously. One minute you're pregnant; the next you're a parent. As carefully as you may have prepared for the transition, you still may be overwhelmed by how quickly it occurs. And you may be overwhelmed by how much you have to *do.* Your body is recovering from the trauma of birth, and your baby is howling for attention. You're expected to adjust immediately, assuming responsibility for its needs as well as your own.

But the postpartum period doesn't have to be all bad. In fact, it has a far worse reputation than it deserves. When I look back at the days after my babies' births, I'm struck by how quickly my life went from rainbows to storm clouds—and back again. I felt raw, I felt ragged, I did my share of grieving, and I often cried at the drop of a hat, but there were just as many times when I felt wonderful and blessed.

One way to stay on top of your postpartum experience is by keeping a journal. Use it to record the feelings, insights, perceptions, and events of the days and weeks following childbirth. Not only will this be therapeutic, it will also be a treasured remembrance of a very special period.

With the hope that my story will help you prepare for your own, I'm including here portions of the journal I kept after Zoe was born. Reading them may give you some idea of what to expect. Then again, your postpartum weeks may prove very different from mine. What's important is to enter this period with a positive attitude.

Why shouldn't it be one of the best times of your life? Never again will your baby be so fresh and new; never again will you have this perfect chance to make a good start together.

DECEMBER 6 ◇ *day one:* Thank God—Zoe is born! Even though she was two weeks late, today seems like Thanksgiving. But the waiting was worth it now that she's here.

The birth was an ordeal. I can't understand how some people can forget what contractions feel like, although I know why they'd want to. My body feels like it's just been through a war. I know I'm bleeding, but I can't get a sense of my lower extremities. Everything aches, and I feel so *very* tired.

Zoe is perfect. Absolutely perfect. I've never seen anything so beautiful in my life. When Gary handed her to me, I cried. She was all wrapped up in white blankets, with just her head peeking out . . . I could have sworn she was looking right at me.

She doesn't resemble either of us very much. She looks more like an ageless being who was dropped from another world into my arms.

I held her for a few minutes, and then the nurse said that she would have to go back to the nursery for a while—the pediatrician wanted to check her over. As we were being wheeled out into the corridor, I leaned over and whispered in my daughter's ear, "There may be a lot of noise and people around, but you don't have to worry. Mommy is here, and I'll take care of you." I loved her immediately and completely.

I was taken to the recovery room, and everyone piled in to congratulate me—my immediate family and a few friends who had been waiting for hours to see the baby. I was glad they came—it was like a big party—but after a while, I wished that Gary and I could be alone.

When I got back to my room, a nurse brought Zoe to me. My parents came in, wearing hospital gowns and masks. I was worried that the masks might scare her (even though the doctor says she can't really focus on anything yet, I don't believe it—I think she *sees*). Since I won't be nursing, I was given a bottle of formula for her first feeding. It had only two ounces in it, but it looked like so much next to her tiny lips. . . . She took the nipple immediately and started to suck, and I felt like the best mother in the world.

After drinking about half of it, she fell asleep in my arms. I drifted away dreaming about graduation dresses and gallons of formula. . . .

THE BONDING MYTH

How you feel during the first few hours postpartum will depend in large part on your birth experience. If everything went smoothly, you may feel elated and proud of yourself. You may be eager to hold and nurse your baby with one hand, and dial the telephone with the other to spread the good news. Or you may want nothing more than to curl up beside your newborn child.

But if your labor was especially difficult or painful, you may be too exhausted to feel excited, and you may not be interested in spending time with your baby right away. If you were medicated, you may still feel out of it—unaware of what's going on around you.

Many women put too much emphasis on this period of time. They think that there's something wrong with them if they don't immediately feel motherly urges. Much of this has to do with what is called the "bonding myth."

"Bonding" has become a sort of catch-all term for the feelings of attachment that develop between mothers and their newborns. It implies a critical time frame, or "window." Missing this window, the myth suggests, may lead to future problems in the mother-child relationship.

But there are many instances when immediate bonding simply isn't possible. A woman may be recovering from a cesarean; a baby may be premature or sickly and require extra days or weeks of hospitalization. And sometimes the traumas of pregnancy and birth take longer to heal.

Gail had a painful and protracted labor. She had to be induced, she had to have an internal monitor, and toward the end, her doctors were seriously discussing the possibility of a cesarean. Her son was almost born in the hallway between the labor room and the delivery room. She had planned to hold him and nurse him right after birth, but she was just too tired. After seeing that he was healthy, she told her husband to take him and fell asleep on the table.

How quickly you bond with your child has absolutely *nothing* to do with how much you love the baby or what kind of mother you will be. Even the ideal childbirth experience takes an emotional and physical toll. You need time to process it and recuperate from it. If you aren't consumed with love for your baby the moment you lay eyes on it, this doesn't signal trouble down the line. Besides, first impressions aren't an accurate gauge of your feelings. Give yourself time, and feelings will follow. Good mothers are made over years and years, not in a couple of critical minutes.

You *will* love your child. (And you *will* think it's beautiful, even if it looks like a miniature version of your Great-Uncle Max.)

DECEMBER 7 ◇ *day two:*   The nurse woke me at 7 A.M. to massage my tummy and take my temperature. So much for sleeping late! Now that I'm a mother, I'd better get used to rising with the sun.

As soon as the nurse left, the pediatrician came in. He told me that Zoe is doing great, and that he'll see us in two weeks for our first office visit.

After breakfast, I decided to get dressed and cleaned up. The journey down the hallway to the bathroom took a long time. I felt weak, shaky, and very unsure of myself. The nurse had recommended a sitz bath, so I settled myself on this funny-looking inner tube beneath the shower. There was a woman next to me who had given birth to a baby boy two days ago. We joked about our stretch marks and decided to call them battle scars. I promised to visit her son in the nursery before going home.

When I returned to my room, a lovely flower arrangement was waiting for me. The card said, "Thank you for our beautiful granddaughter." I started to cry, and it hit me for the first time: *I did it.* I'm a *real* mother with my very own baby!

Then the nurse brought Zoe in and said it was time for me to give her a bath. I was floored. It hadn't occurred to me that I'd have to take care of her in the hospital. Hadn't I done enough already? Why couldn't the nurses do it? I said that I'd watch for now, and promised to do it myself the next time.

The nurse secured Zoe in a football hold with one hand and washed her with the other. The whole process took less than five minutes, but I was shaking and sweating before it was over. Being a brain surgeon seemed easier than holding my slippery baby and listening to her scream.

I was glad when the nurse finally left us alone. While I was giving Zoe her bottle, I had my first chance to really take a good look at her. I furtively unwrapped her blankets and counted her fingers and toes: twenty in all. Then we fell asleep together, and for the first time since going into labor I felt relaxed and at peace. . . .

Tonight I had a lot of visitors. Everyone brought gifts for

Zoe—teeny little outfits (mostly pink), stuffed animals, and the like. Her Auntie Lexa brought a silver picture frame with Zoe's name and birth date engraved on it.

Almost every visitor followed the same routine: They'd walk in, say a hasty hello to me, and disappear down the hall toward the nursery. After about twenty minutes of oohing and aahing in front of the window, they'd come back, exclaim over Zoe, and say good-bye. My friend Cindy was the exception. She arrived with a gift for Zoe, a gift for me, and a genuine desire to hear all about the birth. She brought me a beautiful Mexican smock, smaller than a maternity top but big enough to wear until my body is back in shape. Somehow she knew that I needed something special, too.

Throughout it all, Gary looked proud and happy. He also looked like he needed a good night's sleep. He left early to go home and collapse. We still haven't had a chance to hold each other and talk about our new daughter. Maybe tomorrow. . . .

COPING WITH THE BLUES

The physical experience of giving birth is sometimes compared to running a marathon. The emotional trauma is often equated to what men face when they fight in a war. The combination usually results in what's popularly called the postpartum blues.

At various points during the postpartum period, you may cry uncontrollably and undergo mood swings that leave you dizzy and confused. You may wonder if you're going crazy. You've finally had your baby; shouldn't you be happy and proud? You've waited a long time for this; what's wrong with you?

There's absolutely *nothing* wrong with you. Consider what's happened in your life since conception: For nine months, you tried to imagine what childbirth would be like. During labor, you focused on getting through the next twenty-four hours. Suddenly your baby was out, and in a split second, you went from being pregnant to being a mother—and trying to imagine the next twenty years. No wonder time feels warped and strange. No wonder you can't get a sense of where you are.

The following mental exercise should help bring things back into focus.

- Relive the birth in your mind and remember how you felt at each stage.
- If there were moments in your labor when you were heavily medicated or had limited awareness of what was going on, ask your coach or labor nurse to fill in the missing parts. Try to get a complete picture of the experience.
- Now that you have the full story, tell it to yourself or a friend until you know it by heart.

Recalling the birth can smooth your transition into motherhood.

You'll probably feel extremely vulnerable during the first few days following childbirth, and you may wish that someone would take care of you. This, too, is normal. Your physical and emotional energies have been severely depleted. You need love and nurturing, just as your baby needs to be held, cuddled, soothed, and fed.

Unfortunately, our culture neglects the psychophysical needs of postpartum women. In many other so-called less-developed countries, extensive postpartum rituals have been formulated in response to these needs. People are assigned to massage the new mother, prepare meals for her and her family, take care of her household chores, and help care for the baby. These customs make the postpartum period easier for the woman while celebrating her accomplishment and honoring her status within the community.

More than likely you'll be left alone to care for your baby and everything else, including yourself. While the idea of paternity leave is slowly gaining acceptance, most new fathers spend from a day to, at most, a week at home before returning to work. Dad goes back to his usual routines, and Mom is on her own with her brand-new life and baby. If you're lucky, a friend or relative may cook a meal and bring it over.

The lack of postpartum rituals gives rise to unrealistic expectations on the new mother's part. You may assume that you're supposed to recover quickly and take on your new responsibilities without missing a beat. Visitors may drop in bearing gifts and good wishes, and you'll feel obligated to entertain them. You may not be in the mood to socialize; you may not have the strength to brush your hair. And you may wish that everyone would just go away.

Wouldn't it be nice if people spread their visits out over a couple of weeks, instead of descending en masse? Then you might really welcome an occasional visitor to keep you company and hold the baby. Why not suggest it to your closest friends, the ones most likely to understand?

Meanwhile, take advantage of your hospital stay—the "postpartum honeymoon." This will be your last chance for a long time to beckon someone to bring your meals, give you backrubs, and deliver the baby to your bedside. The shoe will be on the other foot soon enough, and you'll be jumping up at all hours to attend to your newborn's demands.

DECEMBER 8 ◇ *day three:*   Today I got up on the wrong side of the bed. I was crabby and tired, and my body felt as if it had been hit by a truck.

A nurse came in and announced that it was time to "get things moving inside." Apparently I can't go home until I've had a bowel movement. Fat chance! I can't even sit down, much less push. Actually, I'm terrified of the prospect. I'm sure that my stitches will burst or my bottom will fall out. I may have to tell a lie before they let me out of here.

Everything irritates me, including the baby. When the nurse brought Zoe in for her feeding, she was cranky and wouldn't take her bottle. She went back to the nursery without eating, and I can just picture the nurses talking about how inept I am as a mother.

People keep telling me to relax. I wish they'd leave me alone. I'm on the verge of tears, but I'm too tense to cry. And I don't even know why I'm so upset. I'm fine, the baby is fine, but everything seems like too much, too soon. I'm not ready to go home tomorrow. Maybe I could stay an extra day. Probably not. . . .

When Gary came to visit this afternoon, we had an awful fight. It was all my fault. I asked him if the house was clean, and he said it wasn't—no time. I started yelling at him. I told him that babies could only live in immaculate houses—at least, that's the way ours is going to live. He has no idea how tired I am. . . .

By the time I finished my tirade, he looked as if he was ready to cry. The poor guy is exhausted. He's been running to the hospital twice a day, keeping up with work even though he's supposed to be on leave, and doing his best to be supportive. . . .

My best friend came by, too, and she brought me some clothes to wear home tomorrow. I got on the scale and found that I'd lost twelve pounds—only twenty to go. But my stomach looks like layers of crepe paper, and my whole body looks like a deflated version of its former pregnant self. I'm not huge anymore, but it's going to be ages before I can squeeze back into my jeans.

When night finally arrived, I couldn't get to sleep. I kept thinking about what it will be like to go home. I have no experience as a mother. I've never done any baby-sitting, and yesterday was the first time I diapered or fed a baby. Before then, I hadn't even held one for longer than five minutes.

Earlier today Gary kept trying to show me the triangle method of swaddling that the nurses use, but whenever I got two corners in, the third popped out again. I tried practicing with towels in the bathroom, but I still couldn't get it right.

At around midnight, I walked down to the nursery to visit Zoe. On the way, I stopped to look at the babies in the high-risk nursery. Some of them seemed no larger than my hand, and my heart went out to the parents of these infants who are struggling bravely to hold on to life. . . .

When I reached the regular nursery, I stood outside the glass wall and stared at my sleeping daughter in her bassinet (third from the wall and two over from the door). The teddy bear she'd gotten from my mom had fallen over onto her nose, and I asked the nurse to move it back where it belonged. Some of the other babies were crying, and I hoped that the bright lights and noise wouldn't disturb Zoe's sleep.

I was sure that she'd be better off in her own crib. The
nurses have a lot of other babies to watch over, and they can't
give her their full attention. But I can. I think I'm ready to
take her home.

COUNTING YOUR LOSSES

A large part of the postpartum blues is a reaction to the losses
involved in giving birth—the "perks of pregnancy." They're
real, and they're worth mourning over. Here are the things you
may miss:

- *Your pregnant body.* You may not have enjoyed being twice
  as big as usual, but your pregnant body was special. It put
  you in the spotlight. People noticed you. Now you are no
  longer pregnant, but neither do you have your prepregnancy
  figure back. (You'll feel better about your body if you have
  a few outfits waiting for you at home that you think will look
  good during the next six weeks or so. These should be neither maternity clothes nor your tighter jeans.)
- *Your baby.* You may feel an emptiness or a hole where the
  baby used to be. The intimacy and closeness of carrying
  your baby inside you are gone forever.
- *The attention of your family and friends.* Their focus will
  shift from you to the baby, and they may forget all about
  your needs. Before the birth, you were the star attraction
  and the one to fuss over. Now you may feel left out as grandfather meets grandson or auntie meets niece.

  (Be patient. Your contribution of a child to your family
  may well enhance your status.)
- *The single-minded devotion of your mate.* He may lavish
  you with love and appreciation for the gift of life you've
  given him—or he may be so excited from attending the birth
  and meeting his child that he'll barely notice you.

  Besides, he may think you're well taken care of, lying in
  bed surrounded by nurses and well-wishing friends. The
  baby will seem far more vulnerable and in need of its dad-
  dy's big, strong arms.

  (There is something you can do about this. Speak up!)

- *The attention of strangers.* Pregnant women evoke feelings of warmth and respect; mothers are a dime a dozen. Claudia Panuthos, in *Transformation Through Birth,* notes that new mothers often report that they got more help when they were carrying their baby *in utero* than when they started carrying it in their arms, along with a ton of baby paraphernalia. If strangers notice you at all, they're more likely to comment on the baby than on the fact that you have just given birth.

  (On the other hand, you may be a magnet for other mothers. Take this opportunity to create new networks for yourself.)

- *Your former life and life-style.* The baby's demands will infringe on your time, sleep, freedom, career, romance, and identity. Even if you're planning to employ a full-time nanny or housekeeper, you can count on making some sacrifices in each of these areas.

  You may have had similar feelings of loss when you said your wedding vows. Motherhood, too, requires devotion, commitment, and the promise to love and honor, for better or for worse.

DECEMBER 9 ◇ *day four:*   Going home was like a Keystone Kops routine as we lugged the presents and flowers out the door, said good-bye to the nurses, and got the baby strapped into her car seat.

Gary forgot to bring the special outfit I had chosen for Zoe's homecoming, so she went out into the world for the first time wearing a diaper, an undershirt, and lots of blankets. The fifteen-minute car ride seemed to take forever, and I kept turning around to make sure that Zoe was okay.

When I walked into the house, I felt as if I had returned from a long trip—much longer than three days. I don't feel at all like myself. It's as if I've stepped smack into someone else's life.

Everything looks completely different. Baby decor has taken over the living room, and there's a crib and a changing table where the bookshelf used to be.

It's so quiet here compared to the hospital! Almost *too* quiet. I guess everyone is trying to be nice and leave us alone, but I sort of wish someone would stop by and tell me what to do next.

Because this is Friday night, Gary and I lit the candles and said the *Shabbos* blessings. Then I held Zoe and we lit an extra candle, thanking God for having her in our life.

Afterward she went right to sleep in her crib, to the sounds of her Winnie-the-Pooh mobile. Gary and I just looked at each other in amazement. Maybe this will be easier than we thought. We both stood over her crib, staring at her tiny body and watching her breathe.

I'd like to stay awake all night and keep an eye on her, but I'd better go to sleep. I'm glad to be back in my own bed. Now for a nice, long rest. . . .

DECEMBER 10 ◇ *day five:*   Will someone please tell me that it's not 7 A.M. and I'm not awake? I had just closed my eyes when the fierce, persistent screaming started up again. My daughter may be tiny, but her lungs are good and strong. Her cries remind me of the fire drills we used to have in elementary school.

Zoe woke up at 1:30 A.M. and then at 4 A.M. The first feeding was Gary's; the second was mine. My heart was pounding as I raced down the hall to grab her and carry her downstairs. It takes time to warm the formula, so there was about a three-minute lag between her first cry and popping the bottle into her mouth. I tried singing and talking to her while I changed her diaper, but only the bottle would quiet her. After taking four ounces, she fell sound asleep on my shoulder.

I sat there for a while, rocking back and forth, holding my baby. It was so intimate a moment that it almost seemed as if she were back inside me.

Then it hit me—I had forgotten to burp her! What should I do? If I tried burping her now, she would probably wake up and want to eat all over again. If I put her back to bed, she would probably wake up because she needed to burp. I decided to get it over with. Sure enough, she woke up, burped, and was ready for another round with the bottle. Then, after she drank some more, I didn't know if I was supposed to burp her again. Was I supposed to sit there all night? This time I put her back to bed.

The next thing I knew it was morning, and I'd had a total of three hours of sleep. If this keeps up, I don't know how I'm going to function. It took the rest of the morning to get Zoe fed, bathed, and back to sleep. Meanwhile there's a huge pile of laundry in the hamper and tons of thank-you notes to write. And the meals stored in the freezer will be gone before long. With a baby to care for, how will I get anything else done?

This afternoon, while I was taking a nap, the hospital called to find out whether I wanted a home-care nurse to visit tomorrow. I asked if she would baby-sit, but they didn't seem to get the joke. The last thing I need is some expert coming over to tell me how to mother. All I *really* want is a good night's sleep.

Gary went out for a while, and while he was gone, my mom stopped by. There they were, three generations: my mother, my daughter, and me. For the first time, I understood that the woman sitting across from me had been through all this before. In another time, she had done exactly as I was doing: loving, feeding, and caring for a baby. Me.

Tonight we had an awful scare. At around midnight, Zoe started making loud snorting noises, as if she were having trouble breathing. Gary grabbed *Dr. Spock* and started looking under "B" for breathing, "C" for choking, and everything else we could think of. I was on the edge of panic. Then Gary had a good idea: He called the hospital and talked to one of the nurses in the maternity ward. She asked him two questions: "Is the baby blue?" No. "Is she breathing?" Yes. Then the verdict: "She's okay." We put Zoe back to bed, but I didn't sleep very well. I kept listening with half an ear to the sounds coming from the next room.

I got up to feed her in the middle of the night, and I was so tired that I bumped her head carrying her down the stairs. Then I left her bottle on the warmer too long and squirted hot formula right in her eye. She started to scream and I burst into tears, convinced that my child was scarred for life and would need years of therapy to recover from the trauma.

It was the first time I'd hurt her. I'm sure it won't be the last, and I can't imagine how I'm going to survive all the pains and disappointments in store for her. There's no way to protect her completely, and I guess all I can do is love her. That will be easy. I already love her more than I've ever loved anyone.

DECEMBER 11 ◇ *day six:*   My life is so strange these days. Time seems blurry and suspended, and every minute is filled with caring for Zoe. The only way I can tell night from day is by seeing the morning paper waiting for me on the front steps.

I feel removed from the world and totally immersed in the hours between feedings. My main concern is whether there are enough clean undershirts beside the changing table. One of my friends called today and mentioned the war that's going on in Iran and Iraq; I didn't even know what she was talking about, and I didn't care. It's taking every bit of energy I've got to get through the day.

All I really care about is sleep. My mother-in-law offered to come over and stay with the baby so Gary and I could get out, but the only thing I wanted to do was go to a motel and lie down for a few uninterrupted hours. Even when I do sleep, my whole body is tense, anticipating the next time Zoe will wake me up again.

Despite my fatigue, everything seems to be falling into place little by little. Life bears almost no resemblance to the way it was before, but at this point, it seems as if Zoe has been here forever. I can hardly imagine how we lived without her.

Tonight was a very special night: Zoe's great-grandmother came over for dinner. After we ate, I placed my daughter in my grandmother's arms, and she sang her the lullaby that she has crooned to every one of her children, grandchildren, and great-grandchildren: *"Ai-lilli-lu lu, mein Ellen Sue's kindt, Ai-lilli-lu lu, mein Ellen Sue's kindt."* The ancient melody and soothing words brought tears to my eyes as my daughter was blessed by the matriarch of my family.

COMING HOME

You walk in the door of your home, close it to the outside world, and all of a sudden the baby is *yours*—not on loan from the hospital, and definitely not returnable.

Nothing will seem the same. Your body may feel wobbly, your

house may look smaller (baby apparatus takes up space), your career may be on hold, and your identity may be up for grabs.

Fatigue, middle-of-the-night feedings, and isolation may contribute to an overall feeling of fear and apprehension. Your nightstand may be full of books on child rearing, but even if you have the time to read them (which you probably won't), you'll still feel unprepared for parenting.

If you're nursing, the breast-feeding alone may take up most of your time. Thirty years ago, bottle-feeding was the rage; today, breast-feeding is widely accepted as the preferred option. In fact, it's often seen as the first important test of motherhood.

Because of this, many women feel defensive if they choose the bottle instead; others feel guilty if they try to nurse and fail, or if it takes longer than expected to iron out the difficulties. We've tied too much emotional baggage onto what ought to be a personal, private decision. Nurse if you want to and if you're able; if not, don't let it bother you. Millions of babies (you may be one of them) were raised on bottles and turned out fine.

For women who do nurse, the physical symbiosis and emotional intimacy can provide deep satisfaction. Knowing that you're giving your child the most natural form of nourishment can increase your confidence about the baby's well-being.

On the other hand, until breast-feeding begins to proceed smoothly—and this can take weeks—it adds more pressure to an already harried life-style. You have to structure your diet to meet the baby's needs as well as your own, and you have to care for your breasts to prevent engorgement and cracked nipples. Your mate cannot take turns with you in giving middle-of-the-night feedings. Plus, there's the worry about whether the baby is getting enough to eat. With a bottle, you can tell exactly what the child is eating; with nursing, it's less clear. Most nursing mothers worry inordinately about this issue—until the first time the baby's weighed at the doctor's office, when, more often than not, pride and relief replace the worry.

Some women feel apprehensive about nursing in public, and with good reason: Despite the fact that nursing is not a sexual act, there are still people who get uncomfortable and fidgety around a nursing mother. Some may even be rude about it. Giving in to cultural taboos will severely limit your already diminished mobility. If you're comfortable nursing wherever you happen to be, don't let other people's embarrassment get in your way.

However, you may want to avoid public situations that will add to your stress and tension, at least in the beginning. During the first few days, you'll need to be as relaxed and confident as possible when you pick up the baby to nurse. You'll be learning a new skill, and that always takes time, energy, and self-assurance.

If you intend to breast-feed, a little advance planning can make a big difference to your nursing experience. You may want to get some support and/or encouragement—or maybe just some good, sound information. Try:

- The La Leche League—a structured support system available in most communities.
- The hospital where you give birth—it may offer breast-feeding classes to be attended before the baby is born *and* others to be attended during your hospital stay. In addition, some hospitals provide a hot line for breast-feeding mothers who have questions or problems once they return home.
- Your pediatrician.
- Either or both these excellent books: *The Womanly Art of Breastfeeding* (a La Leche League publication), or *Nursing Your Baby* by Karen Pryor. Read these books *before* the baby arrives, and then keep them nearby for quick reference.
- Friends who have nursed.

The postpartum period gives you the opportunity to get to know your child and learn its needs. The consistent demands of the newborn provide you with plenty of opportunities to give it your full attention and figure out the meaning of every little cry and expression.

You wouldn't spend hours standing over your husband and

staring at him while he's fast asleep, yet that's exactly what you'll do with your baby. You'll chart how many ounces of formula it consumes or how long it nurses, study the color of its bowel movements, and try one schedule after another. After the first week, you *will* be an expert, based simply on the hours you've spent observing your child.

Your biggest problem will be lack of sleep. Unless your baby sleeps through the night, giving you the chance to rest fully and recover your energy, you'll feel the strain. Your physical reserves will be depleted, and you may feel crabby, resentful, and incapable of dealing with even the smallest demand.

There are two things to remember about postpartum fatigue. The first is, *it will pass.* Most babies start sleeping through the night by the time they're three months old, and some begin as early as two weeks. As soon as that happens, everything seems much easier.

The second is, *you deserve your rest*—whenever and however you can get it. Eight straight hours may not be possible, but the baby will sleep at various times during the day, and you should take these opportunities to relax. Even if you can't go to sleep, lie down and close your eyes for a while. Forget about the laundry and the house. Take care of yourself first.

Finally: *every* mother has moments of doubt and exhaustion during this postpartum stage—and most survive!

AT-HOME SUPPORT

Many new mothers have someone come and stay with them for the first few days after the baby is born. Often this is an excellent idea, but sometimes it's an awful one. Here are some issues you may want to consider.

Who Should Come?

Mothers or mothers-in-law are the most popular—or at least most common—choices. They can be a joy or a pain, depending mostly on the emotional tenor of your relationship.

You know best which category your own mother or mother-in-law fits into. If you can count on her to be supportive and uncritical, then by all means roll out the red carpet. Her years of experience, combined with a genuine desire to smooth your way into motherhood, may deepen the bond between you.

On the other hand, if she's bossy, overcritical, or interfering, beware! Most new mothers are extremely sensitive about their skills and abilities. If you suspect that your mother or mother-in-law will stand over your shoulder telling you what to do, don't give her the opportunity. Ask her to wait a few weeks before showing up on your doorstep with suitcase in hand. Simply tell her that you need time to adjust.

Becoming a parent may cause a lingering problem or unresolved conflict to rear its ugly head. The postpartum period is *not* a good time for dealing with unfinished business or worrying about other people's feelings. You have every right to refuse to engage in arguments, and outsiders should understand that you may have trouble focusing on anything but the baby.

What you need is someone around with whom you can let down your hair—not someone with whom you have to stand on ceremony (or, even worse, someone you have to wait on or entertain). Whether it's your mother, your mother-in-law, a sister, or a friend, the person who comes to stay with you should be unconditionally accepting and willing to give.

When Should They Come?

If your family lives in another city, they may want to come as soon as possible. Some grandparents are satisfied with a snapshort for a short while, but most are eager for an immediate hands-on experience.

Sometimes it's fun to have out-of-town visitors see the baby immediately following the birth. On the other hand, if you deliver in a hospital, it may make more sense for them to wait until you go home.

Some women like their families or a very close friend to come during the first week. Especially if your mate is going right back to work, you may appreciate the extra help around the house. Then again, this will mean sacrificing some of your privacy. You and your mate will be busy adjusting to the baby and to each other as parents; you may want to give yourself space before sharing this passage with others.

Why Should They Come?

There's only *one* good reason for anyone to stay with you during this postpartum time: to help! That doesn't necessarily include helping with the baby, although you may appreciate someone else watching it while you nap or take a shower. A visitor's main goal should be relieving you of other chores so you can concentrate fully on yourself and the baby.

This means cooking meals, doing laundry, shopping for groceries, and running interference when other people call or drop in. Grandparents in particular may have a hard time sticking to these tasks instead of lavishing their attention on the baby. Establish guidelines ahead of time, if it's at all possible. Discuss your expectations and outline the role you want visitors to play. Be *very* specific about the kinds of assistance you think you'll need, and set the tone when the time comes. If what you need most is for someone to prepare or deliver meals to you during your first week at home, then say so.

If you're comfortable accepting help, people will usually be comfortable giving it. Be assertive about your boundaries with the baby, and others will most likely respect them.

DECEMBER 12 ◇ *day seven:*   One week, and we're all still here. A milestone.

Gary went back to work this morning, and then it was just me and Zoe. This is the first time I've been alone with her for an extended period, and I have to admit that I'm somewhat nervous. What if something goes wrong? I don't even know how to get the car seat into the car, and I probably shouldn't go to sleep in case I don't hear her if she cries. . . . That's ridiculous. How could I not hear her cry? Just the same, I think I'll take her into my room and try to sleep with her next to me on the bed.

While we were napping, my mom came by to drop off a dress for Zoe to wear tomorrow. It looks like a doll's dress. It's for a special occasion: Zoe's baby naming. In the Jewish religion, the birth of a son is traditionally celebrated by a ritual *bris*, or circumcision; in the same spirit, we will welcome Zoe into the family and the community with a naming ceremony that Gary and I have created.

This evening I had an attack of the postpartum blues. Everything was going along just fine when suddenly I felt horribly depressed. It all had to do with the Little Girl Charm.

Early in my pregnancy, I saw a woman wearing a necklace with a gold charm in the shape of a little girl. I coveted that charm, and it became for me a symbol of motherhood, a sort of medal of honor. I told Gary that I wanted one as a gift for giving birth. I found out where they were sold, told him the name of the store, and asked my friends to remind him to buy it for me.

The charm never came. In the excitement of Zoe's birth and bringing her home, I forgot all about it—until today. Within a matter of minutes, I had gotten over being depressed. Now I was furious. Tears streamed down my face as I stormed into the living room to confront Gary. I told him that he'd done something terrible, and that I might not ever forgive him for it. He looked stricken and asked what was wrong. Then, when I reminded him about the charm, he burst out laughing!

Soon I was laughing, too—in between sobs. Gary swore to buy the charm tomorrow. But somehow it didn't seem to matter as much anymore.

We had a hard time getting Zoe to sleep. She kept crying, and we took turns walking her around in circles. Whenever we tried putting her down in her crib, she'd stay quiet for a few minutes and then start screaming again. Her diaper was clean, she definitely wasn't hungry, and we finally decided that she was overtired and would have to cry herself to sleep.

We left her room, agreeing to give it ten minutes. Meanwhile Zoe screamed and screamed until it sounded like she was choking. Gary and I sat on the couch clutching each other and repeating, "Good parents help their children go to sleep." She finally stopped crying, and we collapsed into bed.

EXPECTING CHANGE

Most of this book has been about the changes that occur in your body and your life during pregnancy. Some of these end when the baby is born. And then, much to your surprise, they're replaced by a whole set of brand-new ones.

Change is the main reason for your postpartum feelings of instability and craziness. For almost a year, your life revolved around your pregnancy and its routines. Now your days are filled with endless feedings and mountains of laundry. Sleep seems a thing of the past.

Before your baby was born, you answered to yourself, and your schedule was dictated by your hours at work and your social obligations. Now there's no question about whose needs you answer to and whose schedule you're on. When the baby cries, you run. When it sleeps, you try to grab a nap. In between, you try to squeeze in everything else you have to do.

You may wonder if you'll ever have things under control. Believe it or not, you will. In six months or less, you'll be able to make a phone call, prepare a meal, and fold laundry while making funny faces at your baby, safe in its swing or playpen. You'll be amazed at your own efficiency.

Meanwhile, it may seem as if you've put your identity on hold —or even lost it. You used to be able to carry on a stimulating conversation; you used to have a sex life; you used to read the Sunday paper on Sunday morning, not Thursday afternoon. You used to have friends, but they're off to work and you've started new relationships with soap-opera characters. Your sense of self-worth used to come from feedback at work or your weekly paycheck; now it's measured by whether you got the baby down on the first try.

If you're on maternity leave, you may feel nervous about the work piling up on your desk. You may continue to work from home or stay in touch with the office, either from necessity or to assuage your anxiety. Fatigue can make it very difficult to concentrate, and you may resent having to think about anything but the baby.

Try to be realistic from the outset. Keep to a minimum any commitments you make to your employer, since you won't know in advance how you'll be feeling. If you must maintain regular contact, set up specific, scheduled times when you'll accept calls and carry on business.

Remember that at least some of the pressure you sense will be of your own making. Don't let yourself be trapped into believing that motherhood is in direct conflict with having a career. Lots of mothers work, and many of them actually enjoy their jobs. You needn't feel defensive about your right to recover, spend this special time with your baby, and then go back to work if that's what you want to do or must do.

Caring for a baby all day long can be boring and lonely. Even the most fulfilled stay-at-home mothers have moments when the thought of dangling one more rattle is more than they can take. Isolation can become a serious problem.

The good news is: there are other women out there who are experiencing the same changes as you. Find them! If you're starved for adult conversation, look around your neighborhood for mothers with small children. I was very fortunate; my two next-door neighbors both had children the same ages as mine, and we formed an instant support group. Sometimes all it takes is knowing that you're not alone.

DECEMBER 13 ◇ *day eight:* Today was Zoe's baby naming. We held the ceremony at my mother's house, and all our friends and relatives came. It was the first time that many of them had seen her, and when I walked into the room, I felt like the Queen Mother bearing the royal child.

A hush fell over the room as the rabbi began reciting the traditional blessing. Zoe's grandparents and godparents all had special parts to say, and Gary and I together said a prayer that our daughter would grow up to be healthy, strong, loving, and proud. There was a lot of love in the room, and I saw more than a few tears (and cried some myself).

Throughout the ceremony, Zoe was wide awake and sat in my lap like an angel. Afterward, everyone wanted to hold her, and I got a little upset watching her being passed around from person to person. Finally I asserted myself and took her into the bedroom, where I planned to put her down for a nap. But there was too much noise, and I had to give up and bring her out again.

By the time we got home, she was so exhausted that she fell right to sleep. Then I indulged in a brief bout of the blues. Not the postpartum blues; these were different, related to the ceremony we'd just been through.

Having a child draws all your family and friends together for a while, but in the end it's just you, your mate, and the baby. Mostly I was struck with the sadness of passing time, which I'd felt as I saw Zoe next to my two aging grandmothers. I am no longer the baby of the family, and my grandmas are slowly slipping away. At least they're both here now, for which I'm grateful.

As each new generation begins, another moves aside to make room. Life seems so short; that's why every moment counts.

REAPING THE REWARDS

Just as you're starting to think that one more diaper change will push you over the edge, your baby does something that makes it all worthwhile. The first smile, or the first time it firmly grasps your little finger in its fist, and you stop in your tracks to marvel at the great gift you have received.

The postpartum period is a mix of highs and lows. The feelings of joy and wonder are every bit as intense as those of sadness and apprehension. Your tears are as much a reflection of what you have gained as what you have lost. And right in the middle of everything—the changes, the adjustments, the hard times—is the baby. Nothing in the world is as soft, as sweet, as precious as a brand-new baby, especially when it's yours.

You'll spend hours staring in fascination at that tiny creature, wondering how anything so small could be real. The feeling of a newborn peacefully nestled in your arms will be indescribably delicious to you. Babies are babies for only a short time; when your newborn becomes a toddler, you may yearn for the pleasure of cuddling your baby close. Do it now!

You may be moved to tears more than once by the miracle that is your child. Looking at my own babies, I often asked myself how anything so beautiful could have come out of me. It seems unbelievable that one life could flow so naturally from another. And the best part is: this is only the beginning.

DECEMBER 14 ◊ *day nine:*   A friend of mine once said, "When I take my baby to the supermarket, I carry more stuff with me than my grandparents brought over from the Old Country." Now I know exactly what she meant.

Today was Zoe's and my first solo outing. Our destination was the grocery store, and the whole trip, from beginning to end, took three hours.

At 2:00 I was dressed, Zoe was fed, and everything was packed. The diaper bag was stretched to the limit with three diapers, two changes of clothing, a pacifier, a full bottle, wet-wipes, and dolly.

I managed to get everything out to the car and Zoe strapped into her car seat. It wasn't easy; she kept slipping down until the blanket covered her face. When she was finally settled, I climbed into the driver's seat and reached into my purse for the keys. They weren't there. I had left them in the house.

Was I supposed to unstrap Zoe and bring her along? If I left her alone and ran real fast, would a speeding car come screeching around the corner and crash head-on into mine? Would a stranger take the opportunity to leap out of the bushes and kidnap my child? Should I lock the car doors, or not? Would Zoe start screaming the moment I disappeared from sight?

She sat there contentedly while I wrestled with my fears. Finally I decided to leave her there while I dashed back to get the keys. Before I left, I turned on the hazard lights.

When I got back into the car, we started off. Zoe was in the back seat, and I couldn't see her in my rearview mirror, so I carried on a nonstop one-way conversation all the way to the store. "How are you doing, Zoe? Fine. Is everything okay back there? Sure. Do you like riding in the car? It's great."

Just as we pulled into the parking lot, she dropped off to sleep. Now what? Was this a brief snooze or the beginning of a two-hour nap? Should I curl up in the front seat and go to sleep, too? If I woke her up, would she start screaming, and would I have to feed her in the middle of the grocery store? Maybe I should forget the whole thing and go home.

I looked at my watch. Three o'clock. An hour had passed since we first left the house, and I hadn't even started shopping. I decided that we'd gone too far to turn back. I scooped Zoe up in my arms, grabbed the diaper bag, and marched into the store.

The first thing I noticed were the babies. There were babies everywhere. Somehow I had expected mine to be the only one. Everyone would move aside, offering me the best cart, the first pick of the fresh vegetables, and the front of the checkout line. But three out of four shoppers were accompanied by at least one child, and the only attention I received was when a woman in the bakery department remarked on how handsome my little boy was. I could have killed her. "She's a girl, you idiot," I muttered under my breath. How could anyone make such a stupid mistake?

As I shopped, I looked at the other women pushing their carts and tried to imagine what their lives were like. Most of them appeared to be stay-at-home moms, and every one seemed to have this shopping business down to a perfect science. They somehow managed to squeeze the melons and find the generic brands while simultaneously supervising the children's relay races up and down the aisles. And I could barely handle one sleeping baby, safely ensconced in the front of my cart.

When I finally reached the checkout counter, I was shocked to find that the bill was almost twice what I usually spent. Along the way, I had grabbed several items that we don't even eat—and few that we do. I had frozen veal parmesan and coconut chip ice cream, but no milk, coffee, or bread.

By now it was 4:00—another hour gone!—and I didn't have the heart to return for the staples. I wrote out a check, picked up Zoe, and turned to see how many bags there were.

Then I realized my big mistake. Instead of going to our local luxury grocery store, where someone puts your bags in your car for you, I had chosen the do-it-yourself supermarket. Its motto: "Save a lot of dough—bag before you go."

My groceries were still sitting on the counter in piles. Four people in line were glaring at me to hurry up.

Still holding Zoe, I started indiscriminately throwing things into bags, praying that the eggs would end up somewhere near the top. Eight bags and two lost cans of peaches later (they rolled off down the sidewalk), Zoe and I were back in the car.

I turned on the ignition and she woke up screaming, hungry for her bottle. I drove until I couldn't stand it any longer— three blocks. Then I pulled over into a gas station, changed her diaper on the back seat, and fed her.

When we were finally on the road again, I was surprised to find myself in bumper-to-bumper traffic. I glanced at my watch: 5:00. Rush hour. And 2:00 had seemed like such a safe time to go to the grocery store!

Back home again, I handed Zoe to Gary and announced that I was going to bed. He could unpack the car, put the groceries away, and figure out dinner. I'd had it.

Lying in bed, I was exhausted—and as proud as if I'd just climbed Mount Everest. I learned an important lesson today. Life doesn't stop when you have a new baby; it just takes twice as long!

MANAGING YOUR TIME

Time is what you have the least of once your baby is born. Gone are the days of spur-of-the-moment shopping trips and spontaneous outings with friends, leisurely dinners and telephone calls, and half-hour showers. There's barely enough time to do the things you *have* to do, much less those you *want* to do.

You set your clock by the baby's feedings, and when it finally falls asleep at night, you're too tired for anything but bed. Caring for the baby takes up your waking hours, and those seem shorter than ever.

What's the key to keeping your sanity? Time management. It works in business, and it can work for you.

Successful time management has two parts: *setting priorities* and *getting organized*. Here's how to go about approaching each.

Setting Priorities

The best way to do this is by making lists—preferably two separate ones, in this order:

1. A list of everything you need to do for the baby in a typical day. Brainstorm and write down whatever comes to mind. Include feeding, dressing, diapering, and bathing the baby, plus doing the baby's laundry. Don't forget playing and cuddling. Then, when you think you're finished, put this at the top: *"Take care of myself."* To be fully capable of meeting your child's needs, *you* must be nourished and rested.

   Beside each item, write down the approximate time it takes. Total these and write your total at the top of the page. Then figure out how much time you have left over. (Remember to leave time for you to sleep.)

2. A list of everything else you need or *want* to do that isn't directly related to caring for the baby. At the top of this page, write the time-left-over figure from your first list.

   Then include talking with your mate, seeing your friends, housework, errands, catching up on your reading, preparing meals, and so on. Write these down in order of their importance.

This process should give you a realistic picture of what you can accomplish in a given day and what you can put off until later (or forget about altogether).

Soon after Zoe was born, a good friend shared with me her personal rule of thumb: Each day, plan one—and *only* one— thing to do besides taking care of the baby. If you manage to get it done, you'll have met your goal. And you'll feel as if your life is under control again.

Getting Organized

Many of these tips come from friends who are experienced mothers. Feel free to add your own.

- Set aside one day a week to do laundry, and stick to it.
- If you are bottle-feeding, prepare the next day's formula each evening and refrigerate it.
- Keep your refrigerator stocked with nourishing snacks. Fresh fruits, cheeses, and vegetables don't take long to prepare.
- Keep the diaper bag permanently packed and ready to go. Put it beside the front door so you'll always know where it is.
- Arrange baby apparatus for maximum efficiency. If your bathroom is large enough, put the changing table there.
- Try to set a schedule of who does what with the baby. Example: you'll bathe it every other day, and your mate can take over in between.
- Sleep in a sweat suit instead of a nightgown or pajamas. That way you'll always be presentable, even if you don't have time to get dressed in the morning. (This may not be your style, but it's worth considering.)

What you'll need, more than anything else, is time to become accustomed to your new life and your new baby. Right now the most important thing you can do, besides recover your full strength, is get to know your child. Everything else can be set aside for later.

This little poem says it all.

The cleaning and scrubbing can wait till tomorrow
But children grow up as I've learned to my sorrow.
So quiet down, cobwebs. Dust, go to sleep!
I'm nursing my baby and babies don't keep.[1]

FOR VETERAN MOTHERS

If you are having your second child, this postpartum period will be different from your first. To begin with, you may never before have been separated from your other child for any length of time. No matter how many children you already have, while you're in the hospital, you may worry about whether they're eating properly, putting their shoes on the right feet, and getting enough attention.

If your mate will be attending the birth, you should make child-care arrangements well in advance. Line up a relative, neighbor, or close friend who can be committed to spending at least one night at your house, or arrange to send your child(ren) out. Turn it into a special event. As you're packing your hospital bag, pack a special suitcase for each child. Enclose a note or a small gift.

Back home again, you'll be faced with caring for a newborn along with your other child(ren). If this is your second child, you may experience some sadness as your firstborn is dethroned. It will never again be just the two of you; from this point on, your attention will be split in several directions.

You'll worry about whether your older child(ren) will take to the baby, and whether you'll have enough energy to go around. Will the newborn be welcomed, or will jealousy provoke tantrums and regression? Read about sibling rivalry ahead of time, so that some of the behavior you see won't seem so bizarre.

During the first few weeks, you'll need lots of help. Here is where friends and family come in. Accept their baby-sitting offers. This is an excellent time for grandparents to take your older child(ren) on a special outing; or ask them to watch the baby for a couple of hours while you go off with your other child(ren). It may be hard to leave the baby, but spending time with your other child(ren) will make the transition smoother. Newborns are comfortable in just about anybody's loving arms.

Eventually, things *will* come together. Before long, you'll be able to nurse or feed the baby, read a children's book out loud, and keep an eye on the stove—all at once. Don't be too hard on yourself over the occasional goof. I once walked into the kitchen and discovered that eight of Evan's bottles had burned to a crisp in the sterilizer while I was giving Zoe her bath.

You've heard about the rewards that a larger family brings, but these may not be immediately apparent. For a while, it may seem as if you and your mate are playing "musical children": you'll move from room to room, feeding the baby here, playing with the other child(ren) there, with scarcely a chance to speak to each other. Be patient. Two or more children demand so much attention that you'll probably end up spending more time together than ever.

Most veteran mothers share a common concern, and you may be feeling it, too: Will you ever be able to love your new baby as much as you love the other(s)? The answer, of course, is yes. Each child is unique. You'll delight in watching your older child(ren) assuming the role of big brother or big sister, and you'll appreciate the beauty of your brand-new baby. Sooner or later, the scales will balance.

HANDLING VISITORS

Earlier we taked about whom to invite to your pregnancy. During the postpartum period, the same sorts of considerations apply.

What you need is help and support; what you don't need is uninvited visitors or unsolicited advice.

Visitors can be a welcome break or a terrible imposition. It all depends on who they are, why they're there, and how they behave. As a new mom, you'll need lots of rest, privacy, and time to adapt to the many changes you're going through. For a while at least, the old rules governing your other relationships won't apply.

This is a time when it's acceptable—even essential—to be selfish about your own wants and needs. You may find it awkward to set limits and assert yourself, especially with people you're close to. Here are some tips to show you the way.

- Ask visitors to call before they come. Remind them *not* to drop in without an invitation, even if it's just to deliver a gift.
- Let them know the best time to visit. Ask them to be flexible. For now, your schedule is more important than theirs.
- Be firm about who may or may not hold the baby. Share your child when *you're* ready, not when others want you to.
- Accept any and all offers of meals, but do not feel pressured to provide food for visitors. You're not running a restaurant or hosting a perpetual open house. If someone is willing to prepare food for you and your family, let yourself be waited on.
- Let visitors know what they can do to help. Most will ask and be sincere about it. If necessary, swallow your pride. During this time, it's not out of line to ask a friend to run to the grocery store or wash the dishes.
- Tell people when it's time to leave. You might enjoy company while the baby is awake, but its nap can also be *your* nap. Don't feel obligated to entertain when you'd rather be sleeping.
- Get a Do Not Disturb sign and hang it on your door whenever you feel like it.

JANUARY 4 ◇ *day thirty:*   When I woke up this morning, the sun was shining and the house was very quiet. Too quiet; not a sound was coming from the hallway.

Terrible images of crib death and kidnapping ran through my mind. I raced to the crib—and there was Zoe, fast asleep and totally oblivious to my hysteria.

I didn't know whether to laugh or cry. Her last feeding had been at 1:30 A.M. She had slept for almost eight straight hours!

That's reason enough to throw a party. But it also represents yet another loss—a progression to the next stage of motherhood. I'll miss our middle-of-the-night times together. Before she was born, I hadn't realized that the house could be so peaceful and still.

My daughter has become so important to me. Life seems infinitely more meaningful now that I'm a mother. The sleepless nights were a small price to pay.

Caring for her has become much easier all around. I can change a diaper with my eyes closed in less than thirty seconds, and I can tell the difference between one cry and another. One kind means that she's lost her pacifier; another, that she's hungry. And sometimes I think she's just trying out her voice.

Tonight Gary and I went to an anniversary party for some dear friends of ours. This was our first real date since Zoe was born, and I couldn't help wondering if we'd have anything to talk about besides the baby. I spent hours trying to decide what to wear, and I ended up with my entire closet on the floor. Those last ten pounds *are* murder to lose.

When Sara, the sitter, arrived, I had to remind myself that she's sixteen years old and has had lots of experience. She didn't look old enough to take care of herself, and I had visions of Zoe screaming in her crib while she talked on the phone all night.

I showed her where everything was and gave her a half-hour lecture on Zoe's idiosyncrasies. "She only burps if she's on your right shoulder . . . this is the dolly she sleeps with . . . her mobile needs to be turned so it plays six times . . . she must never, *never* be allowed to cry." Sara nodded, listening patiently to my speech. Meanwhile Gary stood with one foot out the door. Either he didn't see the panic in my eyes or he really is more confident about leaving our daughter with adolescent strangers.

As I was leaving, Sara said, "It will be okay, Mrs. Stern. Don't worry about a thing." Don't worry? *You* don't worry, I thought to myself. This isn't just any baby! She's special! And what's this "Mrs. Stern" stuff? What am I, somebody's mother?

Now *that* was a strange thought. At first I was taken aback, and then I began to feel good. I *am* somebody's mother!

People often comment on Zoe's resemblance to me, and I think I can see it, especially in her smile—which I saw for the very first time this afternoon. I had to look twice to make sure it wasn't gas, but the second time she did it, I knew I was right. I smiled back, and soon we were playing a new game— really communicating.

Before her birth, Gary and I spent hours poring over baby

books, trying to find the right name. Now that I know my daughter, I understand why we chose "Zoe." In Greek, it means "life." In a very special way, life is just beginning.

It's a good idea to interview one or more baby-sitters *before* the baby arrives. Then you have someone to depend on.

A month before your due date, start gathering names. You may want to ask other mothers in the neighborhood for references—but don't be surprised if they seem reluctant to give you this information. A list of baby-sitters is a prized possession that may take years to develop.

Once you've gotten a few names, conduct interviews. Ask each girl (or boy—boys can be excellent baby-sitters, too) whether she's had experience with infants. Does she have baby brothers or sisters? Does she know how to change a diaper? Is she comfortable handling babies? Does she know basic first aid?

Knowing that you already have a baby-sitter to call on will make it easier for you to make plans to get out alone with your mate, and it's *very* important that the two of you do go on a couple of "dates" during the first postpartum month. For a while, the baby will be at the center of your life. Your mate may feel neglected or even jealous.

You don't have to do anything extravagant. An hour-long walk or a dinner out may be sufficient. You may feel like running to a telephone every five minutes; resist! (Or at least wait ten minutes between calls.) Try to focus only on each other.

11

FROM WOMAN TO MOTHER

A few months ago, I attended my first mother/daughter tea—a Valentine's Day party at Zoe's nursery school. As usual, I cried. Whenever my daughter enters a new stage of life, I, too, complete a passage. And I cry: tears of joy at seeing my child take her place among her schoolmates, tears of sadness at being, as my name tag so poignantly says, "Zoe's mother."

I'm still not used to the fact that my children are my children and I am their mother. It still surprises me when they come running with a broken toy or a heart that needs mending. And each time I find the proper tool, the right words, or the hug that makes it better, I know once again that this is what it means to be a mother.

What do you think of when you hear the word "mother"? What memories does it stir? What hopes? What dreams? How will you feel when your child calls you mommy? And what kind of mother will you be?

CHANGING LIVES, CHANGING ROLES

Today motherhood can be anything we make it. We have options that were not available to our own mothers and grandmothers. It's no longer assumed that we'll stay home full-time and make our children the center of our lives. We can choose that role—or we can choose to continue our careers. We can live in nuclear families or extended families, or we can raise our children on our own.

Having so many options is both exciting and scary. On the one hand, it means that we're free to make decisions reflecting our personal values and priorities. On the other, it means that there's no one path, no predetermined identity for us to slip into. We must now make conscious choices that simultaneously take into account our needs and those of our children.

We have as much latitude in substance as in style. As you approach motherhood, you'll probably give a great deal of thought to your relationship with your child. Arranging the nursery and clearing your schedule for the next twenty years won't be enough. You'll also consider the best ways to meet your child's emotional needs, pass on your values, and prepare your child for life in a complex and troubled world. Some of these are issues your own mother may not have explored.

Child psychology, nonsexist child rearing, and alternative forms of education are modern concepts. So, too, is the idea of going *outside* family history and experience for advice on how to raise a child—and help in doing it. We have access to many resources that did not exist for our mothers: a wider variety of books and magazines, hot lines, support groups, community agencies, courses, professional counselors. We talk more freely than our mothers did about the difficulties of child rearing, and we're not ashamed to admit it when we're frustrated or stuck.

It's an exciting time to be a parent. In our willingness to change and challenge ourselves, we're carving out a new and perhaps better definition of motherhood. But it's not necessarily any easier to live up to than the old one. In fact, it may be *more* demanding.

Yesterday's Perfect Mother cooked the bacon; today's Perfect Mother brings it home *and* cooks it while doing aerobics in front of the stove.

The levels of responsibility and commitment involved are enough to frighten the most confident mother-to-be. You're probably worried about the time, energy, and attention your child will demand. How will you make the necessary adjustments? Will you be able to do it all and have it all? Or will you have to give up your own life in order to be a good mother?

One thing is certain: Motherhood will bring profound changes to all areas of your life. Let's look at some of these.

Your Identity

You may fear that having a child will be so consuming that your identity will be absorbed and lost. But motherhood should *expand* your identity, not claim it.

Trying to live your life through your child is wrong for several reasons. It leads to an unhealthy degree of mutual dependency and makes it virtually impossible to let go when you should. It diminishes your capacity to accept your child for what he or she is. It causes resentment on everyone's part. You begin to see your child as a barrier in front of everything else you want to do; your child senses your frustration and ends up feeling responsible for your unhappiness.

There's no need to sacrifice your dreams in the name of devotion. In fact, leading a full life makes you more capable of giving to your child. It's also the best insurance against future empty-nest syndrome.

Rather than detracting from who you are, motherhood is apt to reveal characteristics and talents you didn't know you had, like the patience of a saint, the wisdom of a philosopher, and the wit of a comedian. You'll discover new skills as you solve complicated algebra problems or assemble a swing set.

We see our best selves in our children's eyes. They're so inexperienced that they're easily impressed!

Your Relationship with Your Mate

Becoming parents will alter your perceptions of each other. It will influence the quantity and quality of the time you spend together. And it will definitely affect your sexual relationship.

Will your mate start seeing you as the mother of his child—and stop seeing you as a lover? It's highly unlikely. Some men are initially put off or inhibited by the unfamiliar images of childbirth and nursing. (One husband told his wife that immediately after observing the childbirth—and especially the blood—he wasn't particularly eager to return to the "scene of the crime.") But many men are moved and even sexually attracted by the sight of their mate giving birth and nurturing a baby.

Will you ever be interested in sex again? No question about it. But it will take time (at least six weeks) before you're ready to resume sexual activities. The trauma of birth and any remaining discomfort may lead you to associate your vagina with pain, not pleasure. If you're nursing, you'll need to integrate these added sensations of motherhood into your identity as a sexual being and romantic partner. Meanwhile, the sheer fatigue that results from caring for a newborn may diminish your appetite and dampen your enthusiasm. The possibility of getting an extra hour's sleep can win out over the most ardent passion.

Physical healing and emotional recovery don't happen overnight. Be patient. But don't use your child as an excuse for avoiding intimacy. If you find that you're constantly claiming a headache, exhaustion, or the fear that the baby will wake up right at the critical moment, you may need to reexamine your priorities and make more of an effort.

Children learn about intimacy from observing their parents openly express affection. Nothing makes them feel more secure than the knowledge that their parents love each other. Your child needs attention, but so does your mate (and so do you). A special night out or an afternoon nap can bring you closer and rejuvenate your desire. When your child is older, a lock on the bedroom door will be a perfectly appropriate way of guarding your privacy.

While your lovemaking may be limited at first by the baby's needs, romance may be heightened by your shared feelings of love for your child. You'll need to make better use of your time, however; you'll have to make love when it's convenient, and not always when the spirit moves you—but you'll learn to appreciate the moments you have.

And you'll have the wonderful opportunity of watching each other grow as parents and people. For many women, their attraction to their mate is enhanced by seeing him as a father. The delight of watching your mate teach his son to walk or read a book to his daughter is as gratifying as making love—without worrying about whose turn it is to get up with the kids.

Your Profession

Is it really possible to combine motherhood successfully with a professional life? A lot of women seem to be doing it these days. Many are also at home caring for their newborns, which is where they want to be. The women's movement has finally come full circle, acknowledging and applauding the value of *both* choices.

Each requires some sacrifices; each raises hard questions. If you decide to keep working, will you miss out on valuable time with your child, or will your child suffer from neglect? If you opt to give up your career, will you be bored, regretful, or resentful toward the baby? Obviously the preferred approach is to integrate your priorities so you can enjoy the best of both worlds.

Unfortunately, that's easier said than done. Having done both —I returned to work after Zoe's birth, but not after Evan's—I can say that neither is the perfect choice and each requires compromises. Some women find that motherhood is their true calling; others get cabin fever. Some sincerely want to work but can't bear to be separated from their children.

It's a tough problem to solve, and often it *can't* be solved— only dealt with on a daily basis.

Your Life-style

Having a baby may turn your life-style upside down. If you're used to spending money rather freely, the cumulative expenses of keeping your child fed, clothed, and comfortable will make you think twice about buying a new dress for yourself or going out to dinner.

If you're accustomed to an active social life, you'll have to schedule events around the baby's needs. You'll make adjustments: staying at home more, going to bed earlier, inviting friends over instead of always going out.

You may worry about losing friends when you become a parent, and it is true that this sometimes happens. There are friends who grow impatient with the lack of spontaneity in your life, or they may resent your focus on the baby. But the ones you are really close to—your enduring friends—will honor your motherhood and adjust their expectations. Then again, you may find yourself making new friends with other people who have children. Parenthood is a great equalizer.

Your Values

Becoming a mother will change the way you view the world. Things that never mattered before will suddenly take on great importance. You may begin questioning your politics, your relationships, and your spiritual beliefs. Inflation, pollution, and the possibility of nuclear war will seem even more threatening as you long for a safe and peaceful planet on which to raise your child.

When your child asks you, "Why does the sun rise?" or "Is there a God?" you'll rethink your own beliefs in order to answer. A child's natural curiosity is a compelling reason to grow; in fact, it's almost impossible *not* to.

Children are our best teachers. Their young, inquiring minds push us to reach further into ourselves—and beyond ourselves. At age two, Zoe asked me, "Why is tomorrow?" I'm still trying to figure out what she meant.

"WILL I BE A GOOD MOTHER?"

Every woman asks herself this question. We wonder if we'll be strong enough, patient enough, and smart enough to educate our children. We worry about whether we'll be financially able to provide for them. And we ask ourselves if we have the experience, wisdom, and spiritual strength to guide them through life.

Over the course of motherhood, you'll make countless sacrifices. As the old saying goes, God only had two hands, so he created mothers. But sometimes you'll need more than two hands. From the first middle-of-the-night feeding to the day your child goes to college (and probably longer), you'll do everything in your power to satisfy his or her needs, often at the expense of your own.

You'll also fantasize about what your life would be like if you'd never had children, and you'll resent the demands parenting places on you. There will be times when you'll do anything to get a sitter, and times when a vacation without kids will seem like the only way to renew your energy and restore your sanity.

At moments like these, it would be nice to be able to turn to a manual for mothers—a list of hard-and-fast rules for doing it right. No one has yet written such a manual because there are no such rules. You'll make mistakes (just as your mother did), and your child will get angry (just as you did). Still, you will always be the best mother for your child. You and your mate will know better than anybody how to understand, protect, and love your child. Trust yourself and be willing to learn, and the rest will come with time.

Much of what I know about parenting has come from listening and talking to other people. Recently I attended a blessing for a new mother. She asked her friends to share their ideas of what goes into being a good mother. In the absence of a manual for mothers, here is their collective wisdom.

1. *Be honest.* The truth, even when it's painful, provides order and security.

2. *Welcome change.* If you're comfortable with it, your child won't be afraid to grow up.
3. *Be accepting.* Your child has a right to his or her feelings, even if they're different from yours.
4. *Be human.* Let your child know that you make mistakes, too. It's impossible to live up to perfection.
5. *Let go.* As Kahlil Gibran once said, "You may house their bodies but not their souls."[1]

There's no question that having a child exacts both emotional and physical costs. When you allow yourself to love, you become more vulnerable. Your potential to experience pain increases as you try to protect your child from disappointments. Whether it's a skinned knee, a bad report card, or a broken date, you feel your child's pain as your own. And your joy is multiplied as you share in your child's happiness.

We can quantify the sacrifices of motherhood: countless diapers, the high cost of baby-sitters, and missed vacations are easy to calculate. But it's impossible to put a price tag on the emotional rewards we receive. They take many forms, and they are usually unexpected.

And always recognizable. You'll know it's worth it when your child makes a new discovery, shares a cookie with a friend, shows you a rainbow—or says for the first time, "I love you, Mommy."

REMEMBERING OUR MOTHERS

When someone says "mother," you think of your own, regardless of how many other women have nurtured, guided, or taught you over the years. While she undoubtedly has her faults, she remains central to your vision of motherhood.

Among women everywhere, mothers are the common thread. I've never met a woman, young or old, from any kind of background, with whom I wasn't able to connect on the basis of our feelings about our mothers. Simply mention the word and there's instant rapport.

Women talk about their mothers with an intense mixture of sadness, humor, anger, and joy. None of their stories are simple, and few are finished. The mother-daughter relationship is so complex that it takes years and often a lifetime to resolve and comprehend.

Whenever I think of my mother, one particular saying of hers rings in my ears: "I hope you have a daughter just like you." All over the world, this litany is handed down from mother to daughter, generation after generation.

What does it mean? Is it a compliment or an insult? Are we supposed to have daughters as wonderful as we were, so we'll experience the pride they knew? Or do they hope that our daughters will be difficult so we'll finally understand the struggles and suffering they endured? The phrase remains ambiguous, and maybe that's best. Left to each of us to interpret, it forces us to reexamine the dense web of feelings that has supported (or trapped) us all our lives.

Our mothers are our best friends and our worst enemies, our staunchest supporters and our harshest critics. We yearn for their approval from the day we are born. We can achieve our career goals, develop fulfilling relationships, and attain considerable self-esteem, and we'll still feel empty if we lack that fundamental confirmation of who and what we are.

Some women say that it takes months to prepare to spend time with their mothers, and even longer to recover from the experience. We devote almost as much effort to choosing the right clothes and the right words prior to seeing our mothers as we do before meeting our lovers. They remain our first source of love, our most primal connection. We are all "of woman born."[2]

As you prepare to be a mother, the images of your own will spring forth. All the best moments and the battles will come to the surface as a mirror that will alternately attract and repel you. Whether these images are filled with warmth, tinged with sorrow, or flushed with rage, you will turn to them again and again as you embark on your relationship with your own child.

Our First Role Models

Consciously or not, our mothers leave an indelible imprint on us. Through example and instruction, they provide our strongest impressions of what a mother is. They are our first role models and our most persistent teachers.

We relate to them as mothers first, even if they are much more. Their careers, hobbies, and other interests fade into the background of our one-dimensional perception.

As newborns, we are incapable of distinguishing our mothers from ourselves. As children, we regard them exclusively as the self-sacrificing meeters of our insatiable needs. As adolescents, we perceive them as tyrants to be rebelled against; we're convinced that they can't possibly comprehend our profound feelings and brilliant insights. As adults, we often view them with pity and disdain, and the intoxication of our newfound independence leads us to believe that our choices are superior to the ones they made.

At each stage, we are blind to the big picture. We continue to see our mothers only in relation to ourselves, never as whole persons in their own right.

For many women, pregnancy is the first time they are willing and able to consider their mothers with some distance and clarity. As their focus shifts from themselves to the child they are carrying, they finally begin to look toward their mothers for information and wisdom.

We are on intimate terms with our mothers' finest qualities and worst faults. Few of us are at a loss for words when it comes to describing our mothers. After all, we've been collecting data and sharing results since our first slumber parties. "You won't believe what my mother did!" is a typical teenage refrain, and it remains part of our conversation no matter how old we get.

We take our mothers on dates with us ("Remember, always bring a quarter for the telephone in case you have to call!"). We bring them along to college ("What would my mother think if she knew what I was doing?"). We even haul them into our marriages ("Can she see that I'm all grown up now?"). Their presence continually influences our beliefs and behaviors. It's only when we're able to abandon the litmus test—"Could I tell this to my mother?"—that we're finally on the road to independence.

When we talk about them to one another, it's with equal measures of lavish praise and harsh criticism. Their faults are usually more memorable. We all have lists of grievances against our mothers; some are short, while others are lengthy catalogs of unmet needs and serious wrongdoing. Needless to say, the criticism goes both ways. Mothers have expectations of their children that are just as high as those their children have of them. As both a daughter and a mother, I finally understand.

Most of the women I know blame their mothers for failing to give them a sense of self-esteem. This may be universal in mother-daughter relationships. The lack of self-esteem is central to most women's struggles to become emotionally healthy; it is also the source of their concerns about being good mothers themselves.

Many of our mothers were guilty of sending us negative messages about our bodies, either through direct communication or loud silences on subjects including menstruation, masturbation, and sexuality. While some of our mothers told us that our bodies were beautiful, the large majority said otherwise or kept quiet because of cultural taboos or their own profound embarrassment.

Women also trace their lack of self-esteem to the never-ending struggle to win their mothers' approval. Years later, they are still ashamed of the one B on their second-grade report card or that lock of hair that was never in place. Our mothers may have had lofty ambitions for our brothers, but they wanted us to be *perfect*. To them, we represented another chance at life, another opportunity to do it right. They needed us to be prettier, smarter, and more accomplished than they were.

Not too long ago, I was seated on an airplane beside a woman in her late sixties who was on her way to visit her daughter and granddaughter. I asked if there was anything she would have done differently in raising her child.

"Yes," she said. "My daughter has told me that she felt pressured by our desires and ambitions for her. We always called her our future Miss America, and now I can see that was a mistake."

Many of us have gone through life searching for the Perfect Gift to give our mothers. Some of us have come close in presenting them with sons-in-law. But for many of us, the gift of a grand-child has been the surest way to win their favor once and for all.

Our mothers affected our self-esteem in other ways as well. Their determination to keep us safe in a dangerous world had the unfortunate outcome of stifling our sense of adventure. While our brothers learned to defend themselves, we were taught to be cautious. They did it out of love, but it left us with a limited belief in our own power and a narrowed range of pos-sibilities.

We got the message through a combination of words and ex-amples. We heard "Stay close to home," and we saw our mothers doing just that, raising the kids and often sacrificing their own ambitions. In their generation, full-time motherhood was the assumed occupation. Some of our mothers would opt for the same choice today, but others are sadly aware of the compro-mises they made.

Whether we remember our mothers as being fulfilled or frus-trated, few of us perceive them as having had the broad oppor-tunities and worldly connections that were available to our fathers. How many were able to leave the kitchen to become airline pilots, auto mechanics, doctors, plumbers, or professors? How often did they go away on business trips, chair important committees (other than the PTA), or rub elbows with prominent people in their communities? They ran the household, but our fathers usually had the final say in disciplining us and making the important decisions.

Even if our mothers had careers, they were still expected to perform the domestic chores and assume the responsibility for our day-to-day needs. When they did have nontraditional roles, they usually felt guilty about them. Women's rights and the no-tion of comparable worth were as far off as moon landings.

Nevertheless, they encouraged us to follow in their footsteps.

As little girls, we were given dolls to dress; as adolescents, we were encouraged to make ourselves up and attract attention from boys; at school, we were shown, in one way or another, that attaining academic honors was secondary to receiving our MRS. degree. Our mothers feared that we would end up spinsters, deprived of the social status and economic security of marriage. Single motherhood was unthinkable; it was a *shonda*—a disgrace.

Today most mothers are proud of their daughters' other accomplishments, but their greatest hopes still revolve around eventually being grandmothers.

Jamie, a thirty-one-year-old who's working on her Ph.D., describes her relationship with her mother:

"She wishes that I would get married and have a child. When I called her to tell her that I had been accepted into the doctoral program, her response was, 'You're not getting any younger.' She gave up her career in order to have me, and she's always regretted it. I would have thought that she'd be pleased about my news, but what she really wants from me is a grandchild."

Despite all this, most women care deeply for their mothers and think of them with affection and respect. They were the ones who gave us physical and emotional security. While our fathers put food on the table, clothes in our closets, and a roof over our heads, our mothers cooked our meals, dressed us, and kept us safe under the covers from imaginary monsters and the whispers of the wind. To this day, my mother is the person I want to comfort me when I'm unhappy or ill. I know that I can count on her to be there when it matters.

We gratefully remember the myriad ways in which our mothers cared: sewing the prom dress she couldn't afford to buy, staying up late at night to make sure we arrived home safely, driving around town to find a bag to match our shoes. And some of us recall incomparable moments of closeness when our mothers commiserated with us about adolescent weight gain or shared in the excitement of our first romance.

We were reflections of them, and if they were guilty of anything, it was of wanting too much for us. They took our lives personally, reveling in our victories and agonizing over our losses.

It's surprising how readily we excuse and forgive their mistakes. Most mother stories conclude with the statement, ". . . but she did the best she could." Maybe we genuinely appreciate our mothers' struggles on our behalf. Or maybe we can't bear to believe that they really didn't love us or just weren't capable of giving us the support and approval we craved.

Some of us suffered terribly as children; some of us still do. Yet it's rare for a woman to break all ties with her mother, regardless of how difficult or painful that relationship was or continues to be. The fact is, we still need our mothers. And we never stop entertaining the hope that someday, somehow, they will love us the way we want them to.

We see in our mothers qualities we admire and qualities we reject. As you begin your life as a mother, you may find ways in which you want to emulate the woman who gave you birth. You'll search for means to integrate her positive features while avoiding her mistakes.

For example, if your mother was very giving, you'll probably attempt to equal her generosity in your treatment of your child. But if she sacrificed too much of herself in the process, you'll be just as determined not to let that happen to you.

Every now and then I meet a woman whose greatest hope is to be exactly like her mother. Her perception of her mother is so unilaterally positive that there's *nothing* she would change or improve. More often, however, I encounter a woman for whom there's no greater insult than "You're just like your mother." In order to have a positive self-image, she must discredit everything about her mother. Sad but true, there are mothers out there whose only value as a role model is to serve as an example of what *not* to be.

You're probably more like your mother than you think. As much as I pride myself on being a free thinker and a woman of the eighties, I catch myself from time to time saying something she would say, word for word. We're different in many important ways, but there are parts of her that will always be part of me.

It's time for your second-to-last journal exercise. In this one, you're to play your mother. Complete each of the following statements as you believe she would.

1. I became a mother because I wanted_____.
2. When I found out I was pregnant, I was_____.
3. As a mother, I was responsible for my daughter's_____.
4. The best thing about having a child is_____.
5. The worst thing about having a child is_____.
6. I express my love for my daughter by/through_____.
7. My daughter would/will describe me as_____.
8. More than anything else, I wanted/want my daughter to have_____.

You're not sure what your mother would say? Ask, if you can. Consider this your chance to find out how she felt as a mother and how she interpreted that role.

Now fill in the statements from your own perspective. Afterward, compare your answers with your mother's.

Are there beliefs and values—and hopes—that you share?

INTIMACY AND INDEPENDENCE

We eagerly await the moment when we can tell our mothers that they're going to be grandmothers. We see this announcement as achieving two important goals: bringing us closer to our mothers, and establishing our independence. We can barely contain our excitement, and we expect our mothers' enthusiasm to match our own.

Sometimes it does; sometimes it doesn't.

Most women are genuinely thrilled at the prospect of becoming a grandmother. They are supportive of their daughter's pregnancy and feel validated by her desire to be a mother. And, of course, they can't wait to get their hands on the baby.

But some women are threatened by a daughter's impending motherhood. They see her as a younger version of themselves, setting sail on an exciting journey. By comparison, they feel old, and they don't like it. They allow fear and bitterness to thwart their joy.

Having children is about the closest we can get to being equal to our mothers. But for some pregnant women, the opportunity to "break free" is one of the benefits of childbirth. Motherhood is the ultimate declaration of independence from the family you grew up in. You hope that your mother will finally give you the respect you deserve. Meanwhile, your status as a mother will enable you to make your own decisions, without explaining or justifying them.

Finally, regardless of the way you now feel, your relationship with your mother will change once your child is born. By some miracle, the daughter she complains about (you!) will give birth to the Perfect Grandchild. And she may be the first one you call and the only one you completely trust to take care of your child.

It will be a learning experience for both of you. Your mother will learn to respect your decisions, and you'll learn to value this warm, giving woman your child adores. As you move from woman to mother, and as she moves from mother to grandmother, you'll see each other differently and perhaps even appreciate each other more.

FOR GRANDMOTHERS-TO- BE

Congratulations—you're about to be a grandmother! How wonderful it must be to see your daughter becoming a mother. It is a fulfillment, an affirmation of yourself, a turn of the circle of life.

Besides your grandchild, you have many new things to look forward to. You may have mixed feelings about some of them. You can anticipate having more in common with your daughter. You can foresee a closer relationship between the two of you.

But you may also sense a coming separation. You may still see your daughter as a little girl, but she will be feeling more grown up than ever with her own child on the way. As she is called upon to make important decisions in caring for her child, she will begin to feel a new independence. And she will expect you to recognize that she is now a mature woman, a mother—just like you.

Your relationship will change and deepen as you swap stories, compare notes, and exclaim together about the child's beautiful features and shining intellect. And then, when you offer advice or suggestions, she may slam the door.

She may complain that you're holding the baby wrong, that you've put the diaper on too tight, and that you didn't mash the banana into small enough pieces. She may lecture you on the benefits of baby carriers, declaim the rights of women to nurse in public, and enumerate the advantages of nonsexist child rearing.

At this point, you may wonder, "Why, after twenty years of experience, don't I know a single thing about parenting, while this totally inexperienced daughter of mine is now the expert?"

Most grandmothers feel the same way. As soon as their daughters become mothers, anything they say is wrong, and they spend more time biting their tongues than expressing their opinions.

This is a temporary situation. Remember that motherhood is brand new to your daughter. Her insecurity and defensiveness make her perceive your helpful suggestions as interference. All new mothers are sensitive to criticism, and they especially want their mothers' approval. As your daughter becomes more secure and confident as a mother, she will begin to seek your advice and appreciate your years of experience.

She'll ask you what you did when she had the colic or wouldn't go to sleep at night. She'll want to know how you handled crying bouts and diaper rash. She'll thank you for your help, and then . . . she may go on to do it in her own way.

Each generation goes about things a little differently, and your daughter will occasionally make decisions that will keep you up at night, wishing *you* were the child's mother. But you're not. You did what you felt was right, and so will she. Just as you did, she'll need to make her own decisions regarding her child's care and well-being.

There will be no question that you love this child and have a real stake in its security and happiness. But you won't love it more than its mother does. You will simply have to trust that she'll make responsible decisions based on her love.

Your relationship with your grandchild will be something to cherish and enjoy. As parents often say, "Being a grandparent is so much easier than being a parent. You get all the love, but without the responsibility." And I've heard grandparents say, "Having a grandchild is our reward for what we went through in raising our own children." Both ring true.

But you'll need to understand that this is someone else's child. Grandparents are notorious for allowing later bedtimes, too many sweets, and not enough discipline. Try hard to back up your daughter's decisions. Try hard not to undermine her authority. In return, you can ask this of her: that she respect your right to develop your own relationship with the child, regardless of any differences of opinion you may have.

A grandparent is one of the greatest gifts we can ever give our children. Those of us who are fortunate to still have our mothers and fathers in our lives feel grateful that our children are fussed over, cared for, and loved in such special ways. And we're aware of the invaluable lessons to be learned in linking the past with the future. Knowing our grandparents means knowing where we came from.

As you prepare for grandmotherhood, believe that your daughter will take your wisdom and carry it with her into motherhood. And then give her your blessing.

YOUR GREATEST WISH

In some ways, you're already a mother. Throughout your pregnancy, you've nourished and protected your child, aware of its movements and engaged in a silent communication with it. When someone asks, "What do you think it is?" you may reply, "I haven't a clue," or "It doesn't matter, as long as it's healthy." But *inside*, you may have a strong sense of your baby's gender and even some specific ideas about its personality.

Have you ever secretly imagined that the child you're carrying is the next Beethoven ("It moves to music!"), Joe Namath ("Those kicks are incredible!"), or Greta Garbo ("You should have seen the ultrasound!")? Do you ever joke about its peaceful disposition or enormous appetite? Most of us attribute all kinds of personality traits to our babies long before they're born.

Fantasizing about your child reveals important information about your own dreams and desires. If you secretly hope for a daughter instead of a son (or vice versa), ask yourself why—and then imagine the opposite. If you would like your child to grow up into a certain profession or life-style, try to discover what's underneath your aspirations.

Would you prefer your child to be a carbon copy of you? Or are you praying that he or she will make up for what you've missed?

When I was carrying Zoe, I envisioned a strong, independent little girl who wouldn't be afraid of anything. I wanted a daughter—a child of my gender—but one who would be all the things that I'm not.

If you're honest about your expectations, you'll be less likely to project them onto your child and more able to accept your child for whoever he or she may be.

For your child has already accepted you. In fact, he or she may actually have *chosen* you. The members of some spiritual communities believe that this is how it works. Children look down from the heavens and pick their Perfect Parents.

All right, you don't have to buy this idea. But if you're still questioning your credentials for motherhood, you may want to consider this possibility—because it may teach you something about yourself.

Why Did Your Child Choose You?

Women seem to know instinctively why they're the perfect mothers for their soon-to-be-born children. Here's a sampling of what they say.

"Laughter. My child knows that she will have a lot of fun in our family."

"My child chose me for my tenderness. He knows that he will be loved and cherished."

"My self-awareness. My understanding of myself will help me to understand my child."

"My child chose me because I've been through so much. I'll be sensitive to her struggles."

"My love of life. My child chose me because she's ready for an adventure!"

What special gifts will *you* bring to motherhood? Did your child choose you for your courage, your humor, your independence, your strength? Have you learned certain valuable lessons that you will be able to pass on to him or her? What *is* it about you that your child can see from his or her perch in the heavens?

Each of us is unique, as special and as distinct as the snowflakes that fall from the sky. Every one of your relationships, and all your personal struggles, have combined to create a wealth of wisdom that you will bequeath to your child. Your knowledge and experience are the best preparation for motherhood and the richest gifts you can bestow.

Will you be a good mother? Of course you will. Why? Because of who you are, and because you care. The thoughtfulness with which you are approaching motherhood is the proof of your love for your child.

I believe that our mothers loved us every bit as much as we

will love our children. But I doubt whether they gave anywhere near as much thought to what's involved in a child's emotional health and happiness as we are prepared to give—as you are prepared to give. We are a fortunate generation. And our children are fortunate, too, because they have us as mothers.

The women who are having children today talk less about wanting to give them material wealth and more about wanting to instill in them a sense of emotional security and self-esteem. And while past generations often had specific ambitions for their children, we are committed to enabling ours to fulfill their potential.

Have you ever asked your mother to describe her greatest wish for you? What did she dream about, hope for, and want you to be? Most of our mothers would say, "I wanted my child to be happy." When we speak about the children we are about to have, we say, "We want them to be confident, loving, and most of all, free."

I've asked myself this question many times. What is my greatest wish for Zoe? For Evan? It isn't easy to answer. There are many things I want for my children—more than I've ever wanted for myself. My greatest wish is for them to accept themselves. I want them to respect their own feelings, and I want them to be sensitive to the feelings of others. I want them to love themselves so they can exist peacefully in the world.

What is *your* greatest wish for *your* child?

Afterword

All stories have a beginning, a middle, and an end. But the final pages of this book can only be written by you.

I feel privileged to have shared in your pregnancy. And I pray that your child will be healthy, happy, and everything you hope for.

In the words of my grandmother, "From my mouth to God's ear."

Chapter Notes

Chapter 4 *Coping*

1. Wendy and Matthew Lesko, *The Maternity Sourcebook* (New York: Warner Books, 1984).

Chapter 5 *Thirteen Weeks: You Made It!*

1. *United Nations Decade for Women, 1976–1985: Employment in the United States,* New York: United Nations publication, July 1985.

Chapter 6 *Getting What You Need*

1. Department of Commerce, Bureau of the United States Census, Washington, D.C.: U.S. Government Printing Office, July 1984.

2. Ibid.

3. T. Berry Brazelton, *On Becoming a Family: The Growth of Attachment* (New York: Delacorte Press, 1981).

Chapter 9 *Facing Your Fears*

1. I am indebted to the work of Elisabeth Kübler-Ross, M.D., *On Death and Dying* (New York: Macmillan Publishing Co., Inc., 1969).

2. Rabbi Harold Kushner, *When Bad Things Happen to Good People* (New York: Schocken Books, 1981).

3. American Society for Psychoprophylaxis, *Infant Feeding and Nutrition* (Atlanta, Georgia: American Society for Psychoprophylaxis, June 1984).

4. Claudia Panuthos, *Transformation Through Birth: A Woman's Guide* (South Hadley, Mass.: Bergin and Garvey Publishers, Inc., 1984).

Chapter 10 *Postpartum: The Bridge*

1. Author unknown

Chapter 11 *From Woman to Mother*

1. Kahlil Gibran, *The Prophet* (New York: Alfred A. Knopf, 1923).

2. Adrienne Rich, *Of Woman Born: Motherhood As Experience And Institution* (New York: W.W. Norton & Co., Inc., 1976).